Larry Montz, Ph.D., &
Daena Smoller

ISPR Investigates

THE GHOSTS
OF
NEW ORLEANS

Whitford Press

A Division of Schiffer Publishing
4880 Lower Valley Rd.
Atglen, PA 19310 USA

Photography Larry Montz, Ph.D.

Copyright © 2000 by Larry Montz, Ph.D., and Daena Smoller
Library of Congress Catalog Card Number: 00-103492

Designed by Bonnie M. Hensley
Type set in University Roman/Korinna BT

ISBN: 0-7643-1184-0
Printed in China

Published by Whitford Press
A Division of Schiffer Publishing, Ltd.
4880 Lower Valley Road
Atglen, PA 19310 USA
Phone: (610) 593-1777 Fax: (610) 593-2002
E-mail: Info@schifferbooks.com
Please visit our web site catalog at
www.schifferbooks.com
or write for a free catalog.
This book may be purchased from the publisher.

In Europe, Schiffer books are distributed by
Bushwood Books
6 Marksbury Avenue
Kew Gardens
Surrey TW9 4JF England
Phone: 44 (0) 20-8392-8585;
Fax: 44 (0) 20-8392-9876
E-mail: info@bushwoodbooks.co.uk
Free postage in the UK. Europe: air mail
at cost.

We are always looking for authors to write
books on new and related subjects. If you
have an idea for a book please contact us.

Dedication

This book is dedicated to my mother, Blanche H. Montz, known through-out Louisiana as a pioneer in the modern Hospitality & Tourism Industry. And to my sister, Sandi E. Montz, who followed in her mother's footsteps as a giant in her field of Intercultural Negotiations. Both continue to inspire me.

Larry Montz

This book is dedicated to my mom, Pamela, who chose New Orleans as the first place for us to meet again, face to face. And to Ruthie, for making me laugh since second grade.

Daena Smoller

Contents

Introduction

No doubt about it, New Orleans is haunted. However, until the 1990s, no substantial professional research had ever been conducted in the city. I originally visited New Orleans for the first time in January of 1995 for a vacation. It was then that I was introduced to Dr. Larry Montz, a professional field parapsychologist who was in the city conducting a six-year study on paranormal phenomena and the application of Psi abilities (the most modern scientific term refering to psychic abilities, including clairvoyance) in the field, for the International Society for Paranormal Research. I was fascinated. By the summer of 1995, I was a full-time ISPR Investigator-in-training and ready to assist in the study of all aspects of field parapsychology. I began as a support investigator during ISPR Investigations and furthered my daily studies as a Ghost Expedition Researcher, which enabled me to conduct over 1,000 paranormal field studies under the direction of the most recognized and televised field parapsychologist in the world.

Dr. Montz, who founded the ISPR in Los Angeles, California back in 1972, has a masters and doctorate in the science of parapsychology and is one of only a dozen professional field parapsychologists in the country. In addition, he is the only full-time field parapsychologist in the United States. He relocated to New Orleans in 1990 to conduct a multi-year research study beginning with his residence in a haunted slave quarter apartment in the Quarter. Word spread quickly throughout the city that a professional parapsychologist was in town conducting research. His presence and work created such a stir in New Orleans that for the next six years, Dr. Montz conducted close to 200 paranormal field investigations. But his focus wasn't only on scientifically analyzing phenomena; he also had a revolutionary goal of studying Psi abilities in the field, or simply put, in haunted environments. In the 1970s, Dr. Montz was the first and only parapsychologist to incorporate people with enhanced Psi abilities into scientific research during professional investigations. Previously, Psi abilities were only studied in controlled laboratory environments. Over the years, Dr. Montz used a variety of investigators with different Psi abilities, and through post-investigative research, he was satisfied with the conclusion that applying Psi abilities in paranormal investigations provided much of the subjective information needed to discover what entity or entities were actually haunting a property, if any. This information was, more often than not, substantiated through the post-investigative research.

But what about the Psi abilities of the general public? How do these abilities manifest in a haunted environment? The question is simple, but was never before addressed—the answer was Ghost Expeditions. In 1993, Dr. Montz rocked the parapsychological community with the introduction of Ghost Expeditions, a revolutionary new research technique which utilized participants from the general public in order to study Psi abilities in haunted environments with ISPR-designed controls. During its three-year run in New Orleans, Ghost Expeditions garnered worldwide publicity and became a must-do activity for tourists and locals alike. Ghost Expeditions are currently conducted exclusively in Los Angeles.

Ghost Expeditions in New Orleans provided the ISPR with an additional bonus. It allowed continuous subjective and technical studies of haunted properties to be conducted, something that had never been attempted and has not been achieved since. As a result, through Ghost Expeditions, the ISPR compiled years of information substantiating the *what*, the *who*, and the *where* of real hauntings in New Orleans.

But what about the legends? The ISPR covered that too. During Dr. Montz's six-year study, he insisted on investigating the legends of hauntings throughout the city. As a result, it was easy to trace most of the legends back to a fictional book, *Ghost Stories of Old New Orleans,* written by Jeanne de Lavigne and published in 1946. The properties from which these legends stem were also investigated, and they were found to be just that, legends. So, if you're looking for the little naked girl on a rooftop on Royal Street; wailing from the *sealed room* of slaves that Madame LeLaurie tortured; the young woman killed by her dentist; Father Dagobert singing in St. Louis Basillica; the Sultan that sent assassins to chop up his brother and his harem; the Battle of Shiloh still being fought inside the Beauregard-Keyes house; or the Casket Girl vampires at the Ursuline Convent, the only place to find them is in a fictional book or on a ghost/vampire tour.

Legends can be fun but not nearly as exciting as the real thing. During the years that Dr. Montz conducted investigations in New Orleans, he worked on a variety of fascinating cases ranging from the last remaining light aircraft carrier from World War II to Anne Rice's properties, including St. Elizabeth's Orphanage. Numerous properties that were investigated by the ISPR now enjoy their haunted status and profit financially by exploiting the paranormal findings from ISPR Investigations. One such property is the Ashley House which sits behind a hotel on St. Charles Avenue in the Garden District. The house dates back to the mid 1800s and is now used exclusively for special functions like parties and weddings. Two ISPR Investigations of the Ashley House were conducted—the first in January of 1997, the second a month later. During both investigations, the same entities communicated with the investigative team: a former owner of the house who died of a heart attack, twin teenaged girls who were thrilled to speak through two investigators, a little boy searching for his deceased mother, and an elderly woman who prevented two investigators from entering a parlor in the front of the house. The heart attack victim was extremely violent on both occasions, therefore, the Ashley House was never utilized for Ghost Expeditions.

While in New Orleans, Dr. Montz appeared on television, in print, and on radio about his work in the city and coined the phrase, "New Orleans, one of the most haunted cities in America". Because I worked directly under Dr. Montz, I too, got to participate in many interviews. In 1996, a representative from Southwest Airlines, the Delta Queen Steamboat and myself (representing the ISPR in New Orleans), participated in a live interview on the nationally broadcast radio show, *TravelScope Radio*. Each one of us was asked why tourists should visit New Orleans. Southwest Airlines explained that they offered more flights to New Orleans than any other carrier, making it an easy trip for all travelers. The Delta Queen Steamboat representative said how proud the cruise line was to originate in New Orleans, a city fit for all family vacations. I said it was haunted. When the host asked me why I thought there were so many ghosts in New Orleans, I replied, "Look at the history of the city. The original ramparts were built not to keep enemies out, but to keep the people of the new city from escaping. Commerce was built on vices such as alcohol and prostitution. And with such an intense history including city-wide fires, diseases, and of course, all the terrible crimes due to the vices, well, it's easy to see why there are so many hauntings in the city."

It was a simplified answer that didn't exactly win brownie points with the New Orleans Tourist Commission or HSMA. Although there is truth to the statement, we have learned through the years that there are more causes for hauntings than just disease, anger, and revenge, although those are prevalent causes in New Orleans. In fact, each case can be as individual as the entities that haunt.

After the ISPR closed the New Orleans Ghost Expeditions operation on November 1, 1997, the public demanded more. This book is the response to those demands. Combing through the personal notes of Dr. Montz, audio and video tapes of ISPR Investigations, and the files of Ghost Expeditions Data Collection Sheets, this is the first official ISPR registry of haunted properties in New Orleans. So grab a partner and explore the real hauntings and ghosts of the Big Easy.

Bourbon Orleans Hotel

717 Orleans Street

When one thinks of a haunting, one usually conjures the Hollywood image of an old, run-down house, standing ominously upon a hill, lit only by a few strands of moonlight. That's Hollywood. In real life, hauntings take place in any kind of building—even large, fancy buildings, like hotels. Such is the case of the Bourbon Orleans Hotel in the French Quarter.

The Bourbon Orleans Hotel boasts of a rich history. The site has been home to several changes, each reflecting cultural evolutions and making one quite aware of the magnitude of the passing eras.

The property where the Bourbon Orleans Hotel stands today was at one time two separate buildings, an old convent and an orphanage. The building that stood on the corner of Orleans Street and Bourbon Street was built in 1816, next to the first district courthouse and designed by the architect LaTour. Shortly thereafter, the building burned to the ground, and was rebuilt in 1819. This building was the home of the Orleans Ballroom, used for masquerade and Mardi Gras Balls as early as 1823. This was also the site of the Orleans Theater. The theater and the ballroom could be opened up together for larger functions. It has been said for years that the ballroom was home to the infamous Quadroon Balls. These balls were not costume balls, instead, they were dances held for the wealthy white men of New Orleans to give them the opportunity to choose their quadroon mistresses. According to legal records and documents, the Quadroon Balls were not looked upon as a high-society function. Historians of the time, like George W. Cable, speak of Quadroon Balls, but not at the Bourbon Orleans location. Most of the Quadroon Balls or masquerade parties were at the Salle de Conde, between Dumaine and St. Phillip on Chartres Street. Another location, in 1879, was on Bienville, between Burgundy and Dauphine Streets. In the 1850s, the Louisiana Ballroom, at the corner of Esplanade and Victory Streets, hosted Quadroon Balls.

In 1849, a gentleman by the name of John McDonough purchased the theater, the ballroom and the Orleans Coffee Shop. In 1866, the theater was destroyed by fire but the ballroom was saved. In 1872, the ballroom became the First District Court. In 1881, the Sisters of the Holy Cross bought the building called the Orleans Ballroom for their convent. In 1963, the current Hotel bought the existing buildings, and the Sisters of the Holy Cross were relocated to a new site on Chef Mentuer Highway in New Orleans East. The new convent was built exclusively for them as part of the deal in exchange for the French Quarter site. The newer corner buildings were constructed in 1964.

The first formal ISPR Investigation of the Bourbon Orleans Hotel was conducted in 1995, following years of informal investigations. The following is an excerpt from the log of one of the student researchers accompanying the team that night:

The team quickly moved through the main floor lobby as it was crowded and was not conducive to actual research. Instead, the team moved to the second floor where the ballroom exists today. To walk upstairs, one can choose from either side of the double staircase. One of the investigators said right away that the right-hand staircase was original and that the left was added at a later date. This clairvoyant insight was proven to be correct; post-investigative research revealed that the second staircase was added in 1966.

After reaching the top of the staircase, the team walked through another lobby and into the main ballroom through large wooden doors. It was quickly agreed upon that there were no entities present and scientific readings taken throughout the ballroom concurred with the clairvoyant analysis.

While standing in the center of the ballroom, one of the clairvoyant investigators, Michael, said he could easily pick up on the energy from past events and residual images of large formal parties. The energy seemed to feel fairly recent. He explained sensations of upbeat and positive energy, but that it felt like a modern-day event. Shortly after the investigation, hotel management revealed that a wedding reception had just taken place in the ballroom within the last 36 hours. Between the time of the wedding reception and the ISPR investigation, the ballroom had been completely empty of any visitors.

The team moved down the corridor that leads to the hotel rooms on the third floor. As we passed into a new section of the hallway, we were immediately aware of an entirely different feel to the atmosphere. Most of the team felt the electrical buzzing sensation and vocalized the experience immediately. It wasn't long before the psychic image and information became clear for those who could perceive it. Daena, another investigator, insisted that someone was watching us from the rear. And as long as we remained on the third floor, the electro-magnetic readings remained very high, especially when the equipment was backtracked, behind the team.

As Daena was vocalizing what she felt, Michael turned to look behind the team just in time to see an opalescent image of a man wearing a hat and dressed in gray; it appeared to be a uniform. Michael wasn't quite positive until he turned the next hallway corner and at the other end, stood the same figure. The entity was wearing a Confederate officer's hat with crossed rifles in gold. The soldier remained seemingly curious for a while but faded as he walked around the next corner. As the team approached the last exit door, the soldier and the heavy feeling vanished.

Ed, a student investigator, was trailing behind us to take photos and felt slightly uneasy with the knowledge that he was closest to the entity. As this uneasiness became more intense, he said it felt like someone was breathing down his neck. Ed quickly turned, shot a photo, but there was nothing. We continued further down the

The Bourbon Orleans Hotel used to be a
Convent for the Sisters of the Holy Cross.

hallway and turned the next corner. The electro-magnetic readings started to climb. As we neared the doorway to the third floor, an ice machine, without warning, dropped its ice load, and Ed almost dropped the cameras as he jumped backwards. Guess that proves that not all experiences are paranormal...but can be frightening just the same given the right circumstances!

The team proceeded to the fourth floor using the exit stairwell. Overall, the fourth floor energy remained fairly calm until we reached the third corner. As I stood next to the door of a guest suite, the clairvoyant team members claimed to feel incredible emotional energy. The clairvoyants immediately said, "Nun." I moved from the spot as the rest of the team caught up. Their expressions changed as they felt the energy. One of the clairvoyants moved right into the spot where I had been standing and immediately agreed, "Nun." He got the impression that she was terribly regretful about something, something that has not been made clear at this point in time. While this event was taking place, Ed shot several instamatic photos. During the snapping of the camera, the Nun appeared, even more distressed, and vanished. The photos did not develop.

The fifth floor was non-eventful, but on the sixth floor, the Team witnessed an elderly woman with white hair in what appeared to be a light-colored nightgown. She rounded a corner coming toward us, but retreated immediately. Dr. Montz said this was not a residual haunting; this kind of occurrence is frequently noted because of the sheer numbers of guests a hotel may house throughout the years. It is not unlikely for a guest to pass away and continue to remain and/or visit where the last day of life was spent.

The seventh floor, which currently houses three meeting rooms, offered residual energy from a young female entity. We believe this young girl is somewhere between six and eight years of age and frequently roams the building. After interviewing several hotel staff members, we have found numerous reports of guests, as well as staff, who have heard and seen this young female entity throughout the building. Several guests have called the front desk to report the continuous disturbance of a little girl in the hallway, running up and down and having too much fun.

With the conclusion of the initial ISPR Investigation and subsequent research of the Bourbon Orleans Hotel, the team concluded that the hotel is home to four active entities.

After the initial ISPR Investigation of the Bourbon Orleans Hotel, the property was added to ISPR's list of Ghost Expedition properties. In the span of an average week, ISPR would complete 21 field investigations of the property by utilizing Ghost Expeditions. The same entities would often make an appearance to a portion of each Ghost Expedition team, usually wearing the same clothes and behaving in a manner indicative of each entity. On occasion, the

ISPR Parapsychologist Dr. Larry Montz is getting mic'd for his interview on his research of the hotel, for a Discovery Channel special.

paranormal activity experienced really startled, scared, and thrilled Ghost Expedition participants. Here are a few highlights:

A California couple in their mid-forties joined a nighttime Ghost Expedition. When the Ghost Expedition team of participants entered into the Bourbon Orleans Hotel Ballroom, the majority of the group walked across to the windows overlooking Orleans Street. The group was beginning to document atmospheric conditions when the woman from California grabbed a Ghost Expedition researcher by the arm. She could barely speak, and it was obvious

ISPR Ghost Expedition Group getting a *feel* for the Bourbon Orleans Ballroom

that she was frightened—the color was completely drained from her face. The researcher quickly followed the woman back across the ballroom to where her husband was standing, motionless. Upon learning the man's name, the researcher tried verbally to get the man's attention. Yet he continued to look over the researcher's head in the direction of the windows. All verbal attempts at communication went unaddressed until finally, the researcher reached out and placed her hand on the man's arm. He jerked his arm back, and in a strange, high pitched voice, yelled, "I BEG YOUR PARDON!" The researcher apologized but he again ignored her as his gaze returned to the windows across the ballroom. The man's wife tried next. She touched her husband on the other arm and again he reacted in an alarmed state. He called his wife a "hussy" and told both women that they had no reason to be in the same room. He further explained, in a superior tone, that he was waiting for his *gentleman caller*. Needless to say, that panicked the wife and startled the researcher. The wife began yelling at her husband, calling him by his known name, and within a few seconds, the blank gaze gave way to a look of shock upon the husband's face as the color rushed back to his skin. Upon questioning, the husband said he remembered walking up the first few steps of the staircase and then, nothing.

The female entity that this Ghost Expedition participant was channeling was no stranger to the ISPR team or other Ghost Expedition groups. From the information derived through her numerous appearances, she was alive during the one of the many battles of the previous century and was waiting each and every day for her male suitor to return from war. During another Ghost Expedition, the group filed into the Bourbon Orleans Ballroom and seated themselves at round tables after documenting the current atmospheric conditions. The Ghost Expedition researcher began speaking. Within minutes, the female entity made another visit, this time, stepping into a female participant. The female sat down on the carpeted floor and began making sweeping gestures with her hand, along the carpeting. "Such pretty things, such pretty things," she kept saying. The researcher asked her who she was. The entity said, through the woman, "you know who I am, I am always here and he has returned," as she looked up and appeared to be looking at the back of the group.

From one of the back tables, a young man, in his late twenties stood up as if asked to do so. His fianceé jumped to her feet and yelled, "No! He is not your man!" The entity immediately exited the woman's body, leaving her stunned on the floor. The man in the back explained that he had felt compelled to stand up, that he had some connection with the female entity. His fianceé said that she *instantly knew* that her fiancé was the target and that she was immediately overtaken with great jealousy during the event.

During the almost three years that the ISPR conducted Ghost Expeditions through the Bourbon Orleans Hotel, another entity was a frequent visitor, although he did not make his presence known during the first investigation. The entity is believed to be a pirate—a real pirate. Often times, he relayed information telepathically to Ghost Expedition participants, like his name, Raoul. He had been foolish and became involved in a sword fight, which did not end in his favor. Surprisingly enough, the entity was not mean-spirited about his ending, in fact, he was known for making jokes about it, claiming it is the folly of fools to choose to duel. Raoul had quite an affection for young women and proved this more often than not, by goosing younger female Ghost Expedition participants. Male Ghost Expedition participants commonly reacted in a threatened or aggravated manner when Raoul was present.

One night, a group of five women in their early twenties participated in a Ghost Expedition. They had previously stayed in one of the townhouse suites at the Bourbon Orleans Hotel, and when they complained to the front desk of a number of weird experiences they had throughout their rooms, it was suggested that they join a Ghost Expedition to find out more.

The suite in which the women were staying was a two-story suite overlooking Bourbon Street. However, not all the action was outside. They couldn't keep their bathroom door closed, the water in the bathroom sink turned on and off constantly, the main door to the hallway unlocked and opened each time one of the women shut the door and locked it, and their heating unit turned on within minutes of shutting it off. When the women tried complaining and requested a move to a "less active" room, they were informed that the hotel was haunted. This changed their opinion about the haunted suite. With the five women in attendance, their townhouse suite became the focus of that evening's Ghost Expedition.

Employees at the Bourbon Orleans Hotel were not strangers to odd ocurrences. Unfortunately, however, some of those experiences caused employees to seek employment elsewhere, like one professional chef did in the early 1990s. He was working alone one afternoon in the kitchen on the second floor, which services the ballroom for special functions. During his prep work for that night's event, the chef accidentally knocked two pans off the steel table, making a horrendous amount of noise. Aggravated by the accident, he muttered a few explicatives one would not say around one's parents. Immediately, the lights in the kitchen went out, leaving the chef in complete darkness, followed by a swift and very hard slap across his face. Almost instantly, the kitchen lights came back up and the chef stood still, absolutely stunned. He walked over to the sink and looked in the mirror. He was horrified to see one side of his face completely red and slightly swollen. The chef promptly left the kitchen, walked downstairs and into the administrative offices and quit, on the spot.

The activity during most Ghost Expeditions came from four entities: the confederate soldier, the young woman, the nun, and the pirate. It was documented continuously and consistently for almost three years of ISPR investigative studies. The activity from these entities takes place throughout the hotel, from the single rooms to the townhouse suites, from the seventh-floor meeting rooms, to the ballroom. Residual activities are also in abundance throughout the hotel. It is common to hear children crying from empty rooms, a residual event from the days when a section of the Bourbon Orleans Hotel was an orphanage. One may experience drastic drops in temperature, and if you're fortunate, you may have one of the entities manifest in front of you. But don't be fooled by the Bourbon Orleans Hotel's *haunted piano*. You got it! It's just a programmed player piano.

Although rumored otherwise, historical documentation indicates that the Quadroon Balls of New Orleans were never held in what is now the Bourbon Orleans Hotel Ballroom.

———— French Quarter Courthouse ————

Bordered by Royal, St. Louis, Chartres & Conti Streets

The French Quarter Courthouse is a huge building, taking up one full square city block. The courthouse was in operation from 1909 until 1964. After 1964, the building was home to the Wildlife and Fisheries Museum for several years. In the 1990s, steps were taken to renovate the building in order to make it the new Supreme Court of Louisiana. When the funding was lost, only facade renovations had been started, and were never finished.

Several ISPR Investigations, beginning in 1990, have revealed three entities inside the old Courthouse and one outside.

Two of the entities are always seen together; a young white woman in a brown skirt suit and a middle-aged black man in black dress pants and a white dress shirt. According to court documents, they were both key witnesses in a 1930s mafia murder trial. Even though they were promised police protection

French Quarter Courthouse was home to the Wildlife
and Fisheries Museum for more than a decade.

in exchange for their testimonies, both were shot and murdered in the courtroom before they could take the stand. Sightings of these two entities have been documented since the time of their death by workers and visitors of the building.

During the filming of the movie *JFK* at the courthouse, three security guards were standing inside the building at the entrance door on Chartres Street. Two guards were just completing their shift and the third was just about to begin his. As they were conversing around the guard desk at the entrance, one of the guards turned around and saw a white woman and a black man standing at the other end of the hallway. He called out to them, asking what they were doing in the building. The other two guards turned in their direction and also saw the two entities. However, the couple refused to answer the guard. Two of the guards left the desk and started walking over to the couple. As they got closer, the entities turned a corner and walked out of sight. The guards continued down the hallway in an effort to find the couple again, but when they rounded the same corner, the couple was nowhere in sight. The security guards checked all the office doors—each one was locked. As they went back around the corner, they saw the couple standing at the other end of the hallway. This didn't make any sense. When the security guards got closer to the couple again, they yelled for the couple to stay put and began jogging over to them. But as they reached a space within a few feet of the couple, the pair vanished. The guards turned on their heels, and ran back through the building and out the exit onto Chartres Street; they refused to return to their posts.

The third entity, a male, has been encountered during a number of ISPR Investigations. The ghost is seen wearing a white shirt and tie. He has been found many times in the Federal Public Defender's office as well as in the third floor courtroom facing the Omni Hotel on St. Louis Street. On occasion, guests staying in the penthouse suites of the Omni, which stands right across the street from the courthouse, have inquired to the front desk about the man who is standing in the sealed-off building across the street, in the late hours of the night. The guests are usually pretty shocked to hear from the front desk that the building across the street has been closed for years.

This entity has always refused to communicate with the investigators. The inside joke was that the entity surely must have been an attorney, and since no one is paying his fee, he won't speak.

Outside of the courthouse, another female entity roams the property. Most contact with her has been made on the Chartres Street side of the building. At times, while standing on the sidewalk, people have experienced a soft touch on their arm and sometimes hear a woman crying, begging to see her children. Women have appeared to be more receptive to communication with this entity. Out of all the documented experiences in this area over a three-year period, women had more paranormal experiences by a ratio of 3:1.

The courthouse was a favorite Ghost Expedition location, especially in the evenings, for that's when the most obvious paranormal activity could be easily witnessed. Most evenings, Ghost Expedition groups would stand outside of the courthouse on Chartres Street, directly across from the Williams Research Center. More often than not, the group would witness lights turning on and off inside the vacant and locked building. It was not unusual to see shadows of human shapes walking in between the source of light and the window, creating a shadow outline, the same as a live human would create.

On January 3, 1997, the paranormal activity at the courthouse was remarkable. 33 Ghost Expedition participants stood near one of the trees outside of the courthouse, on Chartres Street. Before any information was divulged by the researcher, a participant brought everyone's attention to a light that was going on and off on the third floor. The entire group watched in amazement. Suddenly, one woman in the group began to cry but in the middle of her gush of tears, was shocked at her own reaction because she, herself, was not sad. As the researcher began to explain that she was probably experiencing an empathic episode with the female entity behind the fence, the researcher was immediately silenced by the force of some object striking her right hand. Before she could react, others were struck as well. As a result, thirty-four people went running down the sidewalk, halfway down the city block before they came to a stop. A gentleman in the group accompanied the researcher back to the original spot of the assault, while the rest of the group remained in the safer area. They were speechless as they saw, littered all over the sidewalk, dozens of objects that resembled a cross between pine cones and burrs. They obviously belonged to a tree in the area, but the night was calm with no breeze and no one was in the trees throwing the objects. Thankfully, only the researcher suffered a gash on her right hand.

Today, the French Quarter Courthouse is ocassionally utilized as a film location.

First-floor hallway where Security Guards saw the entities
of the victims who were shot during the 1930s trial.

First floor lobby of the French Quarter Courthouse

Public Defender's Office where the entity of an attorney
was seen repeatedly during ISPR investigations.

The third-floor courtroom has seen better days.

Crescent City Books Store

204 Chartres Street

The original ISPR investigation of the Crescent City Books Store took place on November 7, 1996, after business hours. The property records for this site can be traced back to 1808. However, there were buildings on this site prior to 1808, and the fires of 1788 and 1794, which burned the entire area. 204 Chartres Street (Crescent City Books) was originally part of a much larger lot which included the corner of Chartres and Customhouse Streets (now Iberville). In the 1808 records, the property was sold with the existing buildings. In 1813, the property was sold again and the records note a two-story brick house and dependencies, or other buildings, so we know that there have been many structures on this corner including the area where the book store is located. In 1829, the property was sold to Louis Joseph Pecquet, who built a new structure. The Crescent City Books building was constructed in 1870 as a commercial property, probably as an apparel manufacturer or other related business indigenous of the area.

This ISPR investigation was quite unusual. Upon the team's arrival, there were several entities of children in the book store that were recognized by the team. One of the investigators immediately saw and felt the presence of three children; one on the first floor in the rear, two on the second, about five feet from the windows and three feet away from the right brick wall.

On the ground floor, the first child entity was standing in the corner of a bookcase on the right wall. At this time, the team identified Christopher, a child known to haunt Le Petit Theatre. An investigator also detected the residual energy of an adult male entity that had passed through this floor earlier that day.

When the team proceeded to the second floor, four more child entities were found and identified by name, four more from Le Petit. As the investigators stood witness, several cushions on the different couches and chairs on the second floor moved. In addition, the same residual energy from the male entity was present and noted. After several minutes, the adult male entity manifested.

Electronically, Dr. Montz located several unexplained, high electro-magnetic fields and roving cold spots. Clairvoyantly, the investigators were able to get a description of a white male, around 27 years of age, dressed in a suit, white shirt, glasses and light brown hair. His clothing was indicative of the 1880s. He generated overall positive energy and did not seem to be related to the building or the location but more to the books in the store. The name Vincent was received the strongest by the team. After several minutes, the presence dissipated and the temperature returned to normal.

When the team reached the third floor, used currently as storage, they immediately felt depressed energy, concentrated near boxes and other items that are stored near the center of the room. The heavy energy was due to two deaths on this floor. The first was a black male, in his late thirties or early forties, in dark clothing. He was stabbed in the stomach, ran into this building, and climbed to the third floor before dying. One investigator had a hard time shaking the taste of blood in her mouth, decidedly an empathic episode with this entity. He had no connection to the actual building. The second was a residual of a young white female that overdosed on drugs probably in the late 1960s or early '70s. Following the first investigation, a second was conducted and more information was garnered on this young girl. She was actually murdered with drugs at age twenty. She was seen with a pink tank top, ragged bell bottom pants and dirty, long, stringy hair. The clairvoyants repeatedly got the name of Carol.

The fourth floor or attic of the building is in disrepair. Just minutes after reaching this level during the first investigation, another entity was discovered as the attic temperature immediately plummeted. The entity was an older white male wearing a tan-colored suit, westcott, gold pocketwatch, and glasses. He had salt-and-pepper hair and appeared to be in his late fifties. His energy was positive. Several of the investigators kept repeating the names of Louis and Joseph. Post-investigative research led the team to believe that this entity was indeed Louis Joseph Pecquet, the new owner of the property in 1829. He was a barrister (attorney) around the mid-1800s. He remained present for a few minutes, possibly curious about the team, and then dissipated. The energy then shifted to a negative feel. Two investigators spontaneously developed pressure headaches and felt extremely hot. Simultaneously, another investigator received an image of a great fire and little slave children dying in this location.

Several photographs were taken during each investigation throughout the four floors of the building. Most developed clearly and without anomalies. However, the cameras malfunctioned seven times during the first investigation, all corresponding with the psychic hits. The video tape from the first investigation turned up blank. In addition, the two audio recorders being utilized recorded nothing but static.

Visitors to Crescent City Books can roam at leisure throughout the first and second floors during regular business hours.

Dauphine Orleans Hotel
415 Rue Dauphine

Walk-through investigations are conducted by the ISPR when it is not felt necessary to bring an entire team. Walk-throughs are used more as a fact-finding mission. The first investigation of the Dauphine Orleans Hotel was a walk-through with Dr. Montz and two clairvoyant investigators, Cari and Brad. The following is the transcript of the audio tapes recorded during that first walk-through and the subsequent letter to Richard Benson, the Dauphine Orleans Hotel General Manager.

Walk-through Investigation Transcription

Note: We started at the corner of the property near Conti and Dauphine. The small cottages are still intact and have been renovated. We started the investigation by walking through the area by the pool. Seemed to be an old carriageway. Lynne was kind enough to provide access to us through-out the Dauphine Orleans Hotel. Scientific data collected has been omitted from the following transcript.

Cari: I'm picking up the name very distinctly of Eldrich. Eldrich is somebody definitely uniformed, it could either be a general or a high-ranking officer in the military and, that presence is here. I feel that he has dark coloration, dark hair, beard, dark, tall, thin, kinda hollow, almost looks like Abe Lincoln in a way, that kind of hollowing of the face, hollow eyes. I feel that this is an entity, I don't feel like it's an image or impression, it's an entity. I feel that it's connected to some elicit romantic thing that happened here, an-other woman that had never been married and she was an older woman, never married, I think they had something going on for a long long time. Whoever this woman was that he was involved with, I'm not getting a clear name except that she was very small and dark-haired.

Brad: I'm getting the name Melissa or Marguerite.

Cari: She left, she went away, she went like out of the country, some European country, and this was a place to rendezvous and she never came back. She like died, she never came back, and that's why he's still here. I'd be interested in knowing if there was a train wreck at that time, she died in some kind of train accident.

Note: We walked into the carriageway.

Brad: I feel a cold spot right here—it's male.

Cari: I know, I've got this person here, I've got this man here, because I started talking about him here. Don't come home with me buddy, I don't have enough room in my house.

Brad: He backed off.

Cari: Yeah, thank you. She's still around.

Brad: I can see the gold buttons on his uniform. It's dark blue though, it looks like the war of 1812 type.

Note: This was in the courtyard area near the pool as we walked to the first bungalow.

Dr. Montz: There is a very high EM reading back here. Very active area. This is an electro-magnetic energy field reading that is registering higher than normal on the magnetometer.

Cari: Was there some kind of water tank under here? Or a well under here, something definitely here.

Brad: you feel a body under here...this could be an epidemic victim or maybe something else. I don't know why a victim would be buried here. What's the actual date on this property?

Lynne: Early 1800s.

Dr. Montz: This is prior to that, this area was a ditch when the original French Quarter was built, there was a ditch here at Dauphine and you crossed it to go to the St. Peter cemetery. Later the additional blocks were added to complete the French Quarter to Rampart Street. We have found other areas along here have the same energy of victims from epidemics or being buried here. The 1722 and 1731 maps of the Quarter show the layout.

Note: This was in the walkway through the arched doorway still approaching the first bungalow.

Brad: This is still part of the small ditch, but here's an old plank road or boards on the ground, and I see a girl that fell off of a carriage, an accident. She's a teenager.

Cari: I'm only getting one body here, I see the body curved laying in a ditch.

Brad: Male or female?

Cari: Female.

Brad: That's what I get, around 17 or 18 years old.

Cari: Yes, that's right, I'm trying to get the date. This person was wearing an odd hair style, almost like there's something in her hair, could be Spanish, maybe a lace thing, kind of like an interesting headpiece, it's not a hat, it's more like a band.

Brad: I think around 1760, there was also an old wooden house close to here, small, a wooden adobe-looking place.

Note: Historical records indicate this corner was vacant until the late 1700s.

Cari: We're talking about a really tiny tiny person. She's an adult, but small, 4'10" or something, really small, petite, very thin, very little bones and wrists, child like, but adult.

Note: This is the area right outside the unit currently being renovated near the arch.

Cari: This place is packed.

Brad: You can feel nervous energy, I noticed that when we walked in.

Note: We went into the large unit to the right near the actual corner, 110 room number.

Brad: I see crates and boxes and such stacked here, and like things were stashed, maybe supplies to build the houses or buildings near by.

Cari: I'm getting a name, Severn. There was a death here, I get a murder, not just a fall asleep and not wake up death, but an actual brutal murder. It was related to thieves. The murder was an element of surprise. Has anyone ever said anything about this room?

Lynne: I know we have one ghost here, but not in this area, as far as I know. I have heard reports of activity in the lounge, another bedroom, and in the main building.

Brad: I know there's a man in the main building on the second floor, has black hair, and blue shirt and pants.

Cari: I would feel very funny staying in this room. That's why I asked about anyone ever making a comment about this room. There's a real morbid feeling here in this room, I would not want to sleep in this room.

Brad: A bloody type of event, like the cutting up with a sword or dagger.

Cari: But it happened quickly, I mean really quick. There was a very big element of surprise. Like it happened in an instant. It was a dagger, it wasn't a sword. It was a dagger, it was used to cut up, not down like you would slash someone, a cut upwards.

Brad: I feel that this area was not a house, but a lot where things were stored and stacked.

Cari: I can see what you mean, was there a cover too, like a canopy?

Brad: Yes, definitely, there was like a tarpaulin over the items. Crates and supplies were stacked here and this man was killed walking next to them. This activity seems to be from the 1730s or earlier.

Note: Went outside to another room, second little room with the old hidden fireplace.

Cari: I hear laughter, some kind of drunken laughter, not like family fun, but drunken—like a whorehouse.

Brad: I get a black man, named Melvin, in here.

Cari: Are you getting him quite recent, like twenty to thirty years ago?

Brad: I can't tell.

Cari: I'm definitely getting something like people drinking and partying.

Note: We then met the other staff members. Mr. Benson said, "this was part of the kitchen, as far as we know. See the fireplace? This room was closed up for a long time."

Cari: This lost soul, the General, is following us. He wouldn't go in that room either. There are so many different ones here.

Note: Then proceeded into the carriageway by the weight room.

Cari: Who is this nut case woman?

Brad: Did she just walk through you, just now?

Cari: She just walked through me. Yes, she walked through me, actually just danced through me. She would dance for no reason, just spinning around. She danced in the middle of the day. She was about 20-21 years old, dark hair, wore it out, loose, not pulled back. And horses here...

Brad: This is the same place I got horses before, was this carriageway a continuance to the other one?

Lynne: I think so.

Cari: Well there was this one thing that just danced through me, straight through the carriageway. Like somebody's nutty relative. I don't think she had a prominent place here, she would have been like the late 1800s, when dresses got a little shorter. It's still long, but slightly raised.

Brad: She doesn't seem to be associated with this place.

Cari: she was a character of that time, just a nut. I got the name Jewel, same one Brad got earlier. I think a horse kicked her in the head.

Cari: These entities want to tell us their names. Why are there are so many people here? Elsten, a care taker, short kind of heavy, chunky, older, not real smart. I feel like I'm tripping over people, there's so many.

Brad: It's almost like having a cemetery, not one but so many people and even from different time periods.

Dr. Montz: Remember this area had a ditch. During the settling of the city, people were buried all over the city.

Note: Now into the lounge.

Cari: I get revolvers here, do you get that?

Brad: Yes, I do. A recent shooting, and also longer ago, the rounded-handle type with flintlocks. There was a duel. They shot down the front of the bar, parallel. The second was a robbery, where someone in the bar fired at the man by the current door.

Dr. Montz: Very high EM readings, also oscillating. This wasn't the original layout or something. This house doesn't belong here.

Cari: It was two people firing at each other consecutively.

Lynne: Do you see anyone here in the bar?

Cari and Brad: Yes, there was a man standing by the piano when we came in.

Note: Next, into the small house on the corner, called the Audubon Studio.

Cari: Somebody was called gorgeous, like a nickname or something, almost like a lot of men knew her. That's what her name was, Gorgeous. She was a big woman, like a joke calling her gorgeous. I think she was an owner of the whorehouse, not May Bailey. I think she was small, but this woman was like a bouncer. She was huge, gorgeous was a joke, very well-dressed.

Brad: Yes, well-dressed but loud colors.

Cari: This was also the room where May counted her money. She also had a male partner in this, the business was under her name. Small thin black man, with glasses. May have been her father. She didn't do too much with the business, not paper work, or like that. She hired people to do these things. I think she was street smart, not book smart.

Brad: This corner of the building had crates here too, before the buildings.

This house also had interior walls, has this been changed?

Lynne: we're not sure.

Note: Then we went to the room above the lounge.

Cari: Has anybody ever seen anything in this room?

Lynne: Yes.

Cari: This is a powerful enough entity to be seen.

Lynne: We don't know exactly what this room was used for. This is the room where people have had experiences. They haven't seen them, but have felt them and heard things.

Brad: It is a male, this was a bedroom.

Cari: Yes, a bedroom. This had to do with jealousy and death. Due to jealousy, there is a reason why the male entity is here, kind of a guilt type thing. I think this male entity knocked off a female, due to jealousy and guilt. This could of even been her husband, she had left him and came here, are you getting a black male here?

Brad: Yes, very big, that might be Melvin, the one I saw downstairs.

Cari: He definitely worked with ships or docks, in his late thirties, maybe forty. I got him just walking directly from the docks, right to here, right up here, in the door, and strangled her, choked a woman to death.

Brad: She was sleeping.

Cari: Yes, sleeping, but scantily clad.

Brad: She was a mulatto.

Cari: She wasn't white.

Cari: She was hooking it and her husband found out and found her here and choked her. I also get the name Andette, not Annette, but Andette. He was a big man and grabbed her with one hand and killed her. Have they ever heard like a scuffling or somebody bump into something in here?

Lynne: Well, people have heard voices in here. A tourist also had an experience in here during Mardi Gras. They heard conversations.

Brad: The name I get was Jessie, Jesop, James, something similar, around forty.

Cari: This area gives me a headache. Let's go downstairs.

Note: We went into the main building, to the first floor, room 116.

Dr. Montz: I get a very high EM reading right here, a circumference of about 2 feet in diameter. Very high.

Cari: Do you think it's like a shaft going down?

Brad: Yes, exactly.

Cari: So do I. It almost feels like somebody fell, like a path of somebody falling.

Brad: It's like an energy vortex. Can we go to the room above this one?

Lynne: I'll check, its O.K.

Dr. Montz: This is room 216, same energy in the same place, very high EM reading, shaft of energy passing right through here.

Cari: This energy is swirling here, not negative but intense.

Dr. Montz: This seems to be a lay line, an energy spot or vortex that passes through the earth. Same readings and same place in this room as well.

Note: Left the room, went downstairs to the property across the street from the main hotel.

Cari: Nothing really here, energy pretty calm. Entities pass through here, but nothing significant. Mostly family activity in this area.

Lynne: Probably due to the Herman-Grima family. This was part of their stables and carriageway.

Brad: I think there was a fire here, do you know of any, Lynne?

Lynne: I'll have to check.

Cari: I do feel energy from an old lady, really old, decrepit.

Brad: I do get a white male in this room, 1950s, sleazy, criminal type, black hair, black leather jacket.

Cari: I get him too. He doesn't belong here, definitely a criminal, seems to hide, shifty.

Brad: He's in his late twenties.

Cari: Yes, I get that, black hair.

Note: We then walked to a couple of other rooms, near the pool.

Cari: This is amazing. There are so many spirits here. They come here to visit, really weird, but very calm. They are from different time periods.

Brad: I get the energy to be very calm also, I also hear sounds of horses and carriages.

Cari: the energy here is completely different from the other side.

Brad: The other side is more negative then here, so many walk through here.

Note: Transcript Completion

The following synopsis report accompanied the transcript of the first ISPR walk-through investigation.

July 14, 1995

Richard W. Benson CHA
General Manager
Dauphine Orleans Hotel
415 Rue Dauphine
New Orleans, La. 70112

RE: ISPR Walk-through Investigation

Dear Mr. Benson,

The following is a synopsis of our walk-through investigation for paranormal activity in the Dauphine Orleans Hotel. I have also enclosed a transcript of the audio tape recorded during the actual walk-through.

We found an incredible amount of activity in the older section of the property, the cottages near the corner of Dauphine and Conti. The Entities, or conscious ghosts, roaming the property are as follows:

A soldier, dark uniform, could be War of 1812 or Civil War. He is a General, or other high ranking officer. His name might be Eldrich. He walked with us by the pool area and back through the walkway to cottages.

A woman, white, 20-21 years old, very friendly, a little nutty, very happy, dances around the property, especially in the carriageway in front of the weight room. Her name might be Jewel.

A man, black, 55-60 years old, friendly, just walks around the property, seems to be a maintenance type person. His name is probably Melvin.

A man, black, 40 years old, negative energy, could have killed a hooker here. His name might be Jesop, James, or Jessie.

We also found elctro-magnetic energy of many other people and events that took place here since the beginning of the city. These types of impressions are mostly clairvoyant images. There are two residual hauntings. The activity here is unusual due to the fact that there were many other entities here today, almost like a gathering for some reason. I have investigated other properties where nearby entities will come due to our conducting an investigation.

The four entities above are your resident spirits or ghosts. These are not impressions; they are conscious presences.

We also found one additional entity across the street, male, white, late 20s, 1950s, criminal type, might not be a resident ghost.

The historical records from the Historic New Orleans Collection did not lend any substantial information. The entities we found do not appear to be any of the past owners of the houses on this site. Charity Hospital did own a large amount of property where the main hotel structure stands, but the property was not used by the Hospital. The Cottage on the corner (Audubon Studio), 401 Dauphine, was also used as a saloon and pool hall in 1896. Another Saloon was at 415 Dauphine in 1896. We will continue to do research on this property and will let you know what we find.

I would like to do a second investigation to try and verify the names of the entities as well as garner any additional information that we may find at the time. It was interesting to find this much data in a walk-through.

I'd also like to return and shoot slides of the sections we covered. I will contact you shortly to review the data and answer any questions you might have.

Sincerely,

Larry Montz, Ph.D.
ISPR

Throughout the remainder of 1995 through 1996, Dr. Montz conducted several paranormal investigations throughout the Dauphine Orleans Hotel and its courtyards, and continued to utilize the property as a "testing" site for ISPR clairvoyant investigators from across the country. The Dauphine Orleans Hotel is located on the corner of Conti and Dauphine Streets in the French Quarter. The small guest cottages around the main building have remained intact and have undergone renovations. The main, multi-level hotel building was found to be clear of any paranormal activity during each investigation. Over the years, the hotel cocktail lounge, cottages, and courtyards have been the sites of numerous reported paranormal phenomena by guests as well as employees.

The hotel lounge, May Baily's, is adjoined to the hotel conference facility. On occasion, bartenders have seen the same apparition in the lounge; a white man with gray hair, wearing a white suit and a Panama-style hat. This entity has been suspected of knocking books off the shelves in the cocktail lounge library from time to time. Interestingly, only books that were of a science fiction genre were thrown to the floor, never the classics.

Many reports have been made by hotel guests of Suite 111, located above the bar. Objects have been moved around the room and the front door locks when guests leave it open. A few guests have reported seeing the apparition of a black man inside the suite. Several investigations by the ISPR have supported that this man's name was George.

The cottage, Suite 110, has been documented as another hot spot for activity. The most outstanding event at this freestanding cottage in recent history took place during a September 1995 ISPR Investigation. After the team and the hotel manager had made their way through many of the hotel's cottage suites, using the same electronic master key to open each door, they approached suite 110. The clairvoyants noted that the energy was extremely heavy. The hotel manager tried over and over, but could not open the door with her master key. Finally, Dr. Montz walked up to the door and verbally demanded that the entities move away from the door inside. The hotel manager tried again and the key worked—it opened the door without any trouble. The clairvoyants refused to go inside. Dr. Montz and another investigator, along with the hotel manager, walked through the doorway. The hotel manager flipped the wall switches for the lights, but they failed to work. She continued for a minute, flipping the switches on and off, but it proved nothing. Then Dr. Montz tried. A quick flip to the *on* position and 75 percent of the room's light bulbs flashed like lightning and immediately blew out. No one could make the mistake of thinking that they were alone in this cottage. The weather was hot, and no air-conditioning was on in the little cottage (which should have made it stifling), though everyone inside immediately experienced goose bumps and drastic temperature variations were recorded. Dr. Montz, the investigator, and the hotel manager remained inside the suite for ten minutes while the other clairvoyants stayed outside. One of the clairvoyants popped her head just inside the doorway and began crying. She explained that she saw a residual of three men who had a young couple tied up with ropes on the bed. They were in the process of torturing the couple and the torture would end in their deaths. The clairvoyant investigator was terribly shaken and after readings were documented, the entire team plus the manager left the premises. However, back through the courtyard, Dr. Montz discovered that the investigator who accompanied him inside the cottage was remiss in taking photographs while the documentation was gathered. The team returned to the cottage for their photos to accompany the report that would ensue from the visit. Once again, the key failed to open the door—but that wasn't the biggest shock. More amazing was the status of the curtains attached inside of the door over the window. They were yanked severely to one side. When Dr. Montz again demanded to be allowed back into the room, and the key did in fact open the door, Dr. Montz and the hotel manager were stunned to see that the top valence holding the curtains had been physically pulled out of the wall, including the valence hardware. It was clear that the ISPR team was not welcome in this location.

The soldier from the war of 1812 and the young dancing female have been the two most frequently witnessed apparitions. They appeared most often by the pool. In the same area were residual images of small clusters of people. They appeared to be involved with transactions of goods on the waterfront, not necessarily wartime activities, but trading activities.

The Dauphine Orleans Hotel was utilized at times for *Private Ghost Expeditions*, Ghost Expeditions of four or less participants. All bits and pieces of subjective information garnered during the Private Ghost Expeditions had already been collected and analyzed during previous ISPR investigations.

–Hotel De La Poste & Bacco Restaurant–
316 Chartres Street

This area of the French Quarter has a very long history. The corners of Chartres and Conti have had structures since the early 1700s. There are two lots joined together in an "L"-shaped configuration. The following information pertains to the Conti Street location where the Hotel now has guest rooms and a parking garage.

Various houses and buildings have stood on this location since the 1730s. In 1788 and 1794, fires swept through this block, demolishing everything. In 1804, the lot changed hands in exchange for a combination of cash and a ship called the *Amiable Celeste,* which was renamed as the *Sarah.* By 1816, there stood a large hardware store for carpenters, blacksmiths, shoemakers, and similar craftsmen. During the period of 1816 and 1822, a very handsome house was built on the Conti Street side where the hotel now stands. The two-story brick house contained a store on the ground floor, and upstairs housed the parlor, dining room, and two bedrooms. A two-story brick slave quarter was erected with a connecting balcony to the main house. Another two-story brick structure stood across the rear of the property, which contained a stable and coach house on the ground floor and a storage room above. The paved yard led to another small brick building which functioned as a bathroom.

In 1896, the historical maps indicate that this area was highly industrialized. Included in this area was a molasses manufacturer; a rice mill; warehouses and factories for clothing, horse collars, and brooms; as well as a wholesale grocer and wholesale liquor store. Where the hotel stands today was a furniture manufacturer, lamp company, and the Commercial Warehouse Company which stored molasses, sugar, and rice. There was also a small apartment building that now houses the offices next to Bacco Restaurant, adjacent to the Hotel, built around 1830.

The ISPR Investigation of the Hotel De La Poste was conducted on July 17, 1996 and revealed two entities and several residual images.

The first entity is a Caucasian woman estimated at 30 to 35 years in age. The team received the name Diane. She was seen wearing what appeared to be an eggshell-colored, thin, straight dress (almost slip-like) with a small pattern around the neck. She had reddish-brown hair, but at times it appeared quite light, probably from lightly-colored scarves. She was first located in the offices on the second floor, and was also found to walk the second floor of the hotel. We were informed later that office employees complained of strange occurrences in the office and that activity was also reported on the second floor of the hotel. Her residual energy was later detected in the Bacco Restaurant dining rooms next store, but not upstairs in the restaurant offices.

From a clairvoyant perspective, the ISPR Team detected depressed energy on the third floor of the hotel offices, where an abandoned apartment was found. The apartment's decor was reminiscent of the 1960s. Residual energy was heaviest from the 1940s, however lighter energy was detected from the 1920s. On the second and third floors, the clairvoyants received empathic information of an illness, probably from a fever suffered here during one of the epidemics. Scientifically, the team measured very high electromagnetic fields throughout the building, coinciding with the presence of the female entity.

In the Bacco restaurant next store, residual impressions garnered by the clairvoyants appeared to be from a past stable where horses were held. In addition, the clairvoyants received another glimpse into the past and saw a larger dining room which was open-air at one time, with a small well in the courtyard.

Back in the hotel, in the far corner of the hotel rooms, closest to Conti and Decatur, clairvoyants received images of three young black children that lived in a two-story building which appeared to be a slave quarter. There were two young brothers and their sister, who appeared to be around eight to ten years of age. It is believed that the three died in a fire which accounts for their depressed residual energy left behind.

In the garage of the hotel, unusual electro-magnetic fields were measured in several different areas. When it was noted by the team that the atmosphere was thick and still, the second entity made his presence known. The entity, Gerald, was a black man in his late forties. The clairvoyants first received information psychically that the area used to be a manufacturing plant of some type with large wooden barrels. This was substantiated later in the historical records. Gerald appeared to be responsible for the care of horses in the stable that used to stand on this site. He communicated that he died in a great fire although it was not confirmed if it was the French Quarter fire of 1788 or 1794. Gerald is responsible for making hotel employees and guests feel like they are being watched or experience the sensation of having someone walking right behind them inside the garage. Gerald felt very responsible for the grounds and stable and has stayed to protect the property.

Although the offices of the Hotel De La Poste are closed to visitors, the parking garage is accessible to visitors via Chartres Street. ISPR's Ghost Expeditions used the Hotel De La Poste for 14 months as a clairvoyant testing site.

ISPR's New Orleans Ghost Expedition
———— Office & Courtyard ————
635 Toulouse Street

ISPR's Ghost Expedition office and courtyard in New Orleans proved to be as actively haunted as any property utilized for Ghost Expeditions. The courtyard was beautiful, but often filled with intensely negative energy. Clairvoyants visiting New Orleans from every corner of the globe felt compelled to stop into the offices and tell the ISPR what they felt in the courtyard. The courtyard made a perfect Ghost Expedition site, for it was active with three resident entities. Furthermore, the emotions of blinding rage and deep sorrow have played havoc with the emotions of most visitors to the office. In the courtyard, countless visitors reacted to the negative energies. If the prevailing *feel* of courtyard was noted as *angry* during the afternoon for example, the Ghost Expedition researcher documented how many people behaved in an angry or disturbed fashion. It made a paranormal first—to study a haunted property daily, as well as study Psi abilities recognized and not recognized by the test subjects, and the effects of paranormal activity on the unsuspecting general public. Negative energy and its ramifications are often easier to recognize and document.

Many celebrities participated in ISPR's Ghost Expeditions in New Orleans, like Delta Burke, Drew Carey, Robbi Chong, Jim Belushi, Crystal Gayle, Miller Light Models, as well as James Van Praggh, Anne Rice's biographer Katherine Ramsland, and too many journalists and television producers to mention. Most of today's internet ghost club organizations have participated in Ghost Expeditions before creating their website organizations. The ISPR was responsible for giving New Orleans its current *haunted status*.

The main two-story house bordering the ISPR courtyard faces Royal Street. The office was located in the back of the house, accessible only by traveling through the long courtyard with entry from Toulouse Street. ISPR also had a second office in the back that was not open to the public. The accompanying two-story slave quarter building lined the right hand side of the courtyard. Both buildings date back to the early 1700s. On the ground floor of the slave quarter building, there was a mardi gras supply store. Since that building was affected by the negative paranormal activity, therefore its occupants, researchers documented the behavior of the employees next store. They appeared to be greatly susceptible to the negative energy.

ISPR's New Orleans Ghost Expedition office and courtyard.

When the ISPR took over this property, the courtyard and office should have been condemned. It took almost a month to make it safe, let alone presentable. The first night after acquiring the keys to the front gate padlock and the office door, Dr. Montz and one of the investigators went to survey all the damage at the office and courtyard to prepare for the major restoration project that lay ahead. When all the notes were taken, Dr. Montz and the investigator locked the office door with the key and then padlocked the gate behind them once they were standing back on Toulouse Street. The restoration was slated to begin the next morning at 10 am.

ISPR's New Orleans Ghost Expedition office and courtyard
located on Toulouse Street in the French Quarter.

When Dr. Montz and his team arrived the next day, they unlocked the padlock and walked to the back of the courtyard to the office. They were met with a large shock. One of the six square panes of glass in the office door had been broken. However, the office door was still locked, and the glass had shattered outward, into the courtyard—not into the office as it would have been if the glass had been broken from the outside. The hundreds of shards of glass lay several feet away from the door—PUT BACK TOGETHER LIKE A PUZZLE!

Access to the apartment is also available by entering the courtyard off Toulouse Street and walking up an old wooden, winding staircase. In the early part of the 1900s, a married couple lived upstairs in the building facing Royal Street. The woman was in her early twenties and considered a natural beauty. Her husband, a banker, was a jealous man. The wife always caught the attention of those passing by and one day, the banker could not control his insane emotions any longer. On the second floor, the banker slashed his wife's face repeatedly with a knife. Incredibly disfigured, the wife spent the rest of her days hidden in her apartment until she sought relief through committing suicide in her mid-thirties. The husband was later killed in a bar room brawl. Upstairs, however, at 635 Toulouse Street, the ghosts of the wife who took her own life and her jealous husband still haunt. Numerous witnesses over a two-year period have documented seeing her face with ugly scars, more promi-

James Van Praggh and friend learn more about New Orleans hauntings during a 1996 Ghost Expedition.

nent than any other feature. Others have felt her grasp their hands or felt their hair blow back slightly as she passes.

The husband's ghost is responsible for making the courtyard one of the most negative areas in the French Quarter. The heaviest concentrations of negative energy are easily detected in several areas of the courtyard; in the front by the gates, in the back right-hand corner and at the staircase located mid-way in the courtyard to the left. While the ISPR used the property as an office, ongoing research was conducted each day in the courtyard itself. It was very common to watch visitors walk halfway through the courtyard, making their way back to the Ghost Expedition office, and stop, only to turn around and leave promptly. These documented occurrences coincided with investigator documentation noting that the entity of the banker was on site. Over the years, two ghost tour operators paid voodoo practictioners and dark witches to use ISPR's Ghost Expedition office and the courtyard as target practice in an attempt to drive us from the site. Although the target practice was confirmed, the paranormal activity was related to the entities on site.

In the spring of 1997, the ISPR moved its headquarters back to Los Angeles, California. The Ghost Expedition office remained open until November 1, 1997. For more information on the ISPR and Ghost Expeditions, check out the ISPR website at http://www.ISPR.net.

Drew Carey joins a 1997 Ghost Expedition in New Orleans

At the center of the French Quarter's Jackson Square, the city's oldest section, stands several buildings, including the Cabildo, St. Louis Basilica, and the Presbytere. Each has been the subject of many ISPR investigations; in addition to their own colorful histories, they each have their own hauntings.

The Cabildo was built in 1799 and served as the Capitol of Louisiana. The Louisiana Purchase was signed on the second floor in 1803. The Cabildo, now one of the historic properties used for the Louisiana State Museum, houses one of the three death masks of Napoleon.

The Cabildo's courtyard has what appears to be a slave quarter, but was actually utilized as a prison during the War of 1812. During the war, a young man was hung in the courtyard and his entity haunts the property today.

The paranormal activity began at the same time renovations did, after the Cabildo caught fire in 1988. The museum police reported that they were being pushed in the hallways and down the stairs. Interestingly, this happened only to male officers, not females. That makes sense, taking into consideration just when and where the entity lived while alive. During the entity's lifetime, only men held positions of authority. After the renovations were completed, the detrimental activity ceased. Now, when the Cabildo is rented out for special functions, it is not uncommon for people to experience food and beverage being knocked out of their hands. They all provide the same descriptions of the young man who creates the havoc, but they don't understand why security won't try to find him!

Next to the Cabildo is the oldest active cathedral in the United States, the St. Louis Basilica, located at the head of Jackson Square. However, because of fires in years gone by, it is actually the third cathedral to stand on this site.

Inside the St. Louis Basilica, beneath the floor, over a hundred parishioners found their final resting place. It was thought that one could be closer to heaven if one paid to be buried in such a fashion. Maybe that was true for those buried under the floor, but not so for the Bishop that haunts the cathedral. In current years, many have witnessed the sightings of the Bishop in front of the alter. He does not interact with the worshipers or visitors, he merely watches.

Watching is the favorite past time of the entity who haunts the building next to the St. Louis Basilica, in the Presbytere. He is an elderly man who made a living as a janitor while still alive. He is seen wearing dark uniform pants and shirt, and has curly light-colored hair with a receding hairline in

Cabildo at Jackson Square

front. The entity haunts the Presbytere, one of the many historical properties utilized for continuous exhibits by the Louisiana State Museum. In addition, the janitor visits several of the apartments on St. Ann Street, adjacent to the Presbytere. Female residents complain the loudest about his visits as they usually take place at the most inopportune times—while the residents are in the shower. Don't all janitors appreciate cleanliness?

Running in between the St. Louis Basilica and the Cabildo Museum is Pirate's Alley. Pirate's Alley boasts so many legends surrounding the meetings of Andrew Jackson and the infamous pirate, Jean LaFitte, although those meetings never really took place there. The alley did not exist at that time; in fact, there were buildings where the alley is today. There are, however, two interesting hauntings that take place in this area.

At 624 Pirate's Alley stands a yellow building, Faulkner House Books. While living in New Orleans in this very house, William Faulkner wrote his first novel, *Soldier's Pay*. Next to the bookstore is a beautiful four-story red house. The first two floors contain living rooms, dens, and marble bathrooms. The completely modern kitchen is located on the third floor with the oversized master bedroom and magnificent master bath on the fourth floor. The ghost of a little girl, approximately eight or nine years of age, haunts the house. At times, she can be seen from Pirate's Alley, usually in the third or fourth floor windows. The owner doesn't mind her presence at all.

Traveling further along Pirate's Alley, toward Royal Street, one will come to the back of the St. Louis Basilica. Along the back of the building there is a walkway, perpendicular to the Alley. For over two decades, along this walkway, is a residual haunting of a priest. Those who have seen him describe him as holding an open book with both hands, head down over the book, as he makes his way back and forth along the walk. He never looks up nor acknowledges anyone in view. It is believed that this priest was so intense in his prayers, that his energy was retained in this location, providing us with a glimpse into the past.

St. Anthony's Garden is located behind the St. Louis Basilica on Royal Street. The garden is the highest-elevated point in the entire French Quarter. In the back of the garden, closer to the cathedral, there are three graves. In fact, they are the only below-ground graves in the Quarter. Two graves are occupied, one containing the remains of the very first black Bishop in New Orleans. The third grave is empty.

Some of the French Quarter storytellers will tell the legend of the mass burial in St. Anthony's Garden. The legend is a fabrication of a real event. In the mid-1900s, a ship sailing south of New Orleans docked in Pilot, Louisiana with the entire crew infected with malaria. In Pilot, the crew members died and were buried, and a Pinnacle monument was constructed in their honor. There were concerns about the monument's longevity due to the periodic hurricanes which destroy property throughout Louisiana without exception. The monument was moved to where it stands now, in St. Anthony's Garden, closest to Royal Street.

Note of Interest: During the time that duels were fought between men with swords, many took place in St. Anthony's Garden. When guns replaced the swords, the duels continued until the gunshots made so much noise that the priests demanded that the duels be fought elsewhere. From that point on, duels were fought at City Park, located at the end of Esplanade Avenue. A section of City Park trees are now nicknamed *the dueling Oaks of City Park*.

Cabildo during restorations efforts after the 1988 fire

Ominous skies above the Cathedral at Jackson Square

Interior of the Cathedral at Jackson Square

Presbytere

Jackson Square.

Pirate's Alley

Keuffers, The Slave Quarters, & The Gray
——————————Building Apartment——————————
Corner of Chartres & Toulouse Streets

Often, a haunted property will sit vacant or have a high turnover. The building on the corner of Chartres & Toulouse Streets has been for sale numerous times over the years. Each time it's sold and renovations begin, the construction crews are frightened off the job. Who can work when crew members are being knocked off ladders or tools are disappearing?

For four years, from outside the building, various ISPR clairvoyants as well as participants on Ghost Expeditions have seen a young woman who haunts the property usually standing inside the second-floor windows overlooking Toulouse Street. On three different dates, the shudders were observed changing position at one second-floor window, without any natural explanation like wind or rain. An informal ISPR Investigation was conducted in this property in January 1996.

Upstairs, above the bar, the two large floors were empty except for old French books, a broken register, an old wooden ladder, and pigeons. Residual energy from the female entity was perceived inside the building, but she was not present at the time of the walk-through.

Behind the main structure is a multi-story slave quarter building. Condemned for many years, it is unsafe to visit. However, from the street, while watching the main building, the apparitions of many crying slave children in the window openings facing Toulouse Street have been documented over and over. In addition to the children, a large black man carrying a whip has been seen pacing along the second floor balcony.

In the back of the slave quarter building, which butts up to a parking lot, are several square openings. It was often the practice of Ghost Expeditions to check out the slave quarter building by requesting volunteers to stick their hands into the openings. Over a two-year period, about 30 percent of all volunteers felt their hands grabbed from inside. A word of caution for anyone who plans to visit the building: the slave quarter building is vacant and is not structurally safe to enter.

Across the street from Keuffers, in another prime French Quarter location, a second-floor apartment on the corner above the Stage Door Bar has stood vacant for many years. This is another example of a haunted property that no one wants because of its paranormal activity.

In 1995, the listing real estate agent spoke with Dr. Montz about the apartment. He claimed that in the past, prospective renters would walk inside the door and feel upset, and sometimes actually physically ill. He stated that these prospective renters never made it past the living room.

This apartment is haunted by the entity of a young man in his mid-twenties. He was a gunshot victim, a result of his involvement with drug trafficking most likely in the 1970s. Many people passing by have seen him in the window overlooking Chartres Street, wearing jeans and a white teeshirt. Unless informed, they do not know that they were looking at a ghost.

The most frequent sightings of this entity occur during daylight hours.

Back of slave quarter, located adjacent to Keuffer's.
Windowless openings are rectangular in shape.

——La Maison Marigny Bed & Breakfast——
Faubourg-Marigny District

On July 18, 1996, the ISPR conducted an investigation of La Maison Marigny at the request of the new bed and breakfast proprietor. Lynn had taken over the old house, restored it and opened for business. She hadn't counted on paranormal activity as part of the atmospheric charm. The investigation turned out to be a good time for all; the following is from the log kept by Daena Smoller regarding this investigation.

Lynn, the new owner, explained that she and her guests had experienced a wide range of strange occurrences, like feeling a gentle kiss on her cheek as she laid down in bed, or waking up in the middle of the night to smell eggs and bacon frying, only to find the kitchen void of food and people. One afternoon, a female guest at the bed and breakfast saw Lynn in one of the bedrooms. The guest passed the room and went downstairs. When she entered the living room, she couldn't believe her eyes. There was Lynn, again, watching the television. In the weeks that followed, Lynn hosted a couple, but did not like the man for reasons unknown. On the second night of their stay, the couple was keeping company with Lynn in the living room. The man made some comment that offended her, but before she could react, the man was hit in the head with an empty soda can. No one else was in the house at the time. The couple left the next morning.

Lynn also reported that at all times during the day and night, she and her guests hear someone walking the staircase. And one day, alone in the house, Lynn was bent over the bathtub scrubbing. She was interrupted from her work by a playful pat across her back end. She turned around quickly but nobody was there.

The ISPR investigation began at 5:00 pm. When the team gathered in front of the building, three investigators saw a young girl looking back from the left-hand second-story window. She wasn't alone. The investigators sensed clairvoyantly that there was someone else upstairs in a back room and yet another entity standing just inside the front door. When Lynn met the team at the door, she invited everyone into the front parlor. The equipment was retrieved from its protective bags and the tape recorder was immediately turned on. Lynn began relating various experiences while the investigators became engrossed with the cold air that brushed back and forth between them. Dr. Montz and student investigator Ed could feel something, too. Michael, one of the clairvoyant investigators, was watching something intently. Karen was handling the 35 mm camera and tried to snap off a few photographs, but the camera malfunctioned. Ed grabbed the instamatic camera, but both pictures developed with completely brown screens, no images at all.

Dr. Montz suggested that we move on. As he and Michael walked into the main hallway, they received scientific and psychic hits at the same time. The magnetometer, which measures electro-magnetic fields that are sometimes associated with the presence of an entity, registered a field that sent the needle off the scale. An entity, who later identified himself as Stanley, was standing right next to them. I walked right into Stanley's space and immediately began laughing. No horror here, this was one jovial entity. Dr. Montz and Michael both announced at the same time, "This is Stanley." As they verbalized their discovery, I felt my body go cold with a buzzing sensation from head to toe. I continued to laugh as I moved toward the staircase. It felt like I was following this entity. Without thinking, I said, "eighteen steps, that's a lot of steps to walk." Ed took a photograph of the staircase with an auto-focus camera, but the photo came out blurred. At times, we record anomalies on film like this, in others, a small section of the picture is out of focus. While Ed was taking the photos, Michael counted the steps on the staircase: eighteen.

Upstairs, the hallway runs the length of the house. Two bedrooms to the left with the doors wide open and one to the right and front of the house. As I turned right, something grabbed my
attention from the back bedroom, but Dr. Montz redirected us to the front bedroom. The room had a beautiful decor. The owner began to speak, but I didn't hear a thing she said. I was listening to Stanley. He was communicating in very colorful language that *his* room had been made into something just a little too feminine for him. His happy energy made me laugh—too bad no one else heard the remarks!

A moment later, another entity entered and sat on the corner of the bed. It was the young girl in the window. Possibly 17 or 18 years of age. She seemed oblivious to us; we got the impression that she functioned within her own world when she was alive. She made the meter dance but her energy was dull and unattached. The cameras still wouldn't work and she shortly faded away. We left the room and walked down the hallway to the back bedrooms.

The middle bedroom was non-eventful, but an older woman was in the other. I knew that she was the one that captured my attention at the top of the stairs and was the one that kisses Lynn's cheek as she lays down to sleep. I felt a little sad. Dr. Montz and Ed were recording the meter readings. The sadness dissipated when the woman left the room. We left too and went back downstairs.

The main floor hallway led us through the kitchen, family room, and then outside to the back yard. I sat on a wooden swing and immediately felt Stanley move in between me and Dr. Montz. He remained stationery while Dr. Montz spoke. I recognized four instances of Stanley communicating telepathically as he increased the pressure of his touch.

When we re-entered the house, we moved directly into the kitchen. Karen and Ed continued through the house to take more photographs per Dr. Montz's instruction. All of a sudden, there was this faint smell of eggs and bacon frying. Lynn was the first to speak, "there it is!" It was definitely residual. Dr. Montz explained that since it was such a calm house, mundane residual activities could easily be manifested. This was a good sign. As he spoke, the older female entity from upstairs showed up behind me. My eyes began to well up with tears and I felt like crying. Instantly, my reaction changed and I felt relief instead; the kind one may feel when they realize someone else understands. I could feel this entity's love for Stanley and the young girl upstairs. Then it became clear, clairvoyantly, what had happened to these three people.

Post-investigative research proved the clairvoyant information correct. These three people were a family that once resided in this house. The three unfortunately, died in an auto accident in the 1940s. They remain because it is their house, but they are very fond of Lynn and only interfere with her business a little.

Only a few interior pictures actually developed during this investigation. EM meter readings and temperature fluctuations were taken throughout the house and we registered several simultaneous scientific and psychic hits. Now that Lynn is at ease with her home-mates, she feels no need to take any further action.

Le Pavillon Hotel

Le Pavillon Hotel sits on a piece of land with history as rich as one can find in the city of New Orleans. Originally owned by the Sieur de Bienville (founder of the city), it was then purchased by the Jesuits. After the Jesuits were forced to leave, the land had a new owner, Mr. Jean Gravier. Gravier was a wealthy sugar cane and indigo plantation owner. The property, however, declined to a frightening and dangerous area by the 19th century.

The early 1830s saw the birth of the New Orleans and Carrollton railroad, the oldest in the city. When the railroad depot was no longer utilized, the structure was remodeled to become a showcase for circuses, traveling shows, and other attractions. In 1867, the National Theater, often called the German Theater, was built. In the 1870s, the property was owned by Philip Werlein, founder of the famous music store of the same name, and the theater became known as Werlein Hall. It was destroyed under mysterious circumstances in 1889.

In 1899, ownership of the property went to La Baronne Realty Company. They constructed a hotel soon to be known worldwide for its modern amenities and splendid luxury; the New Hotel Denechaud was completed in 1907. It was the first building in New Orleans to have hydraulic elevators installed, as well as the first building ever in the city to have a basement. Again, in 1970, under new ownership, the hotel underwent an incredible restoration and was renamed Le Pavillon. On June 24, 1991, Le Pavillon was placed on the National Register of Historic Places by the U.S. Department of the Interior.

In August of 1996, management of Le Pavillon wanted to know if the hotel was haunted.

The ISPR Investigation began in the lobby area. We found our first scientific piece of data when we moved into the restaurant dining room. Along the floor, we recorded high electro-magnetic energy fields but later found in the basement that the main equipment for the hotel is located under the restaurant, which generates EM fields of its own through normal operation. Two of the clairvoyant investigators sensed the presence of two entities, a man and a woman, near the buffet tables in the dining room. The temperature around the investigators dropped temporarily. A third cold spot was recorded and remained for approximately 30 seconds.

The team moved to the second floor via the staircase. Here, high electro-magnetic readings were recorded and most of the investigators felt the sensation of heat from a fire. In the hallway of the second floor, the entire team and hotel management experienced a strong sulfur smell moving right through the group of people. The presence of the couple was again detected. An apparition manifested of a young man in a dark suit on the third floor. On the fourth floor, everyone experienced the sulfur smell again. The apparition of the man in the dark suit reappeared on the sixth floor. No unusual equipment readings on the seventh and eight floors; they were clear.

As soon as the team emerged from the stairwell onto the ninth floor, it was unanimously agreed upon that the energy of the hallway was different. It was much colder than the others and the sulfur smell returned. The entity was that of a young girl; she appeared to be somewhere between 16 and 19 years of age. She manifested a long blue dress of empire design from the 1830s or '40s. Her energy was agitated. Eva, Ava or Aida could be her name; it is believed that she died nearby.

The pool area, health spa, and rooftop were all clear during the investigation.

The ISPR investigation of Le Pavillon in August of 1996 revealed five entities. None of these entities are malevolent and do not appear to disrupt operations at the hotel. The investigation, however, did not offer a great deal of substantial scientific information.

Le Pavillon Hotel lobby.

Hallway where paranormal activity was first noted on guest
floors during the initial ISPR Investigation of Le Pavillon Hotel.

ISPR Parapsychologist Dr. Larry Montz and investigators before entering Suite 930.

Dr. Larry Montz taking EM field measurements during ISPR Investigation.

Le Petit Theatre
616 St. Peter Street

Le Petit Theatre is the oldest active theater for continuous live performances in the United States. There are actually two separate buildings here. The first one is located on the corner and currently houses the children's theatre, called Teddy's Corner. On this site, prior to the great fire that swept through the French Quarter in 1788, stood a wooden house for the Bishop. Rebuilt in 1789, this became the home of the last ruling Spanish Governor. The second building, which houses the main stage and auditorium, was constructed in 1922. It was torn down in 1962 and rebuilt in 1963.

Entering the theatre through the Helen Hayes foyer which connects both buildings, one walks on ballast flooring. The material was removed from ships that had docked in New Orleans. No such rocks are naturally found in this area of the United States.

The foyer windows look out at the courtyard, defined by the outer walls of the theatre building complex. The wall and double door exit of the children's theatre lines the courtyard on the left and main theatre exit doors and wall are on the right. Behind the wall straight ahead is the two-story concrete stairwell that leads up to the attic. Non-employees were not usually allowed in the attic, let alone the stairwell or backstage, but Ghost Expedition participants were the exceptions and were thrilled to be so! Most employees, however, wouldn't venture into the attic alone. It was an incredibly active area of the theatre, the subject of numerous ISPR Investigations.

The attic is shaped in a giant "L", one section running the length above the children's theatre, the other section running between the children's theatre and the main stage, above the back stage area of the main auditorium. Over Teddy's Corner the attic houses almost one hundred years of live performance props—including swords, doors, suits of armor, and household goods. The second part of the attic, running between Teddy's Corner and the Main Stage and Auditorium, is the storage area for rows and rows of costumes. This section of the attic opens up over the main stage, hidden from the audience by one of the stage curtains.

Over the six-year period that the ISPR conducted paranormal field research in New Orleans, Le Petit Theatre was a favorite hot spot. Over thirty formal investigations were conducted, as well as three years of Ghost Expeditions. In those six years, eleven entities were documented in the theatre. Six were children.

The child entities at Le Petit Theatre range in age from seven to ten. They come from time periods dating from the early 1800s to the most current,

Helen Hayes foyer entrance at Le Petit Theatre.

Le Petit Theatre as seen from Chartres Street.

1991. Contrary to generations of folklore, entities from different time periods are not on different dimensional planes of existence. In fact, they are in OUR plane of existence and are well aware of one another. Just like live people, they decide if they want to communicate with the other entities as well as living persons. In this case, the children stayed together at all times. They pretty much had the run of the theatre and would interact frequently with Ghost Expedition participants. A Ghost Expedition that was conducted on September 23rd, 1995, had two New York women participating.

When the researcher brought the participants into Teddy's Corner, one of the New York women sat down. She was extremely warm and weak due to the hot temperature and muggy conditions. Suddenly, she felt cold all around her her lap. She screamed through her giggles when she brought the attention of everyone present to rest on her thigh. Without being able to see an apparition, the group witnessed the woman's thigh get repeatedly pinched. The woman admitted that she loves children, which is probably why they were attracted to her.

Ages of the children were deciphered by the clothing that they wore as well as information they communicated. The history behind one of the children, Stephanie, was the easiest to substantiate and validate.

One December night in 1991, the set crew was working behind stage, designing and building new sets for an upcoming play. One of the young female workers began to cry. She said she was terrified and sad at the same time. Two other workers made an effort to walk her out through the backstage exit which opens onto Chartres Street. When they were a few steps away from the exit, all three became frightened and ran back to the rest of the crew, claiming something invisible was blocking the door. The rest of the crew, feeling strength in numbers, went to check out the disturbance. As they neared the exit, each one stopped dead in their tracks; something unseen WAS blocking the door and no one could get close.

During the ISPR investigation that ensued the following day, the child entity Stephanie was found for the first time. Clairvoyants on the team substantiated that the feelings she projects are those of terror and sadness. Stephanie telepathically relayed her story. One afternoon, while outside playing in broad daylight, she was abducted by a large man. In her struggle, one of her shoes fell off her foot. She was taken to a site under a New Orleans bridge where she was raped and strangled to death. Her body was buried under bags of garbage. She provided her last name, her home address and what day of the week it was when her abduction and murder took place. Research through the New Orleans police validated the entity's story. Not only was Stephanie's shoe found where she said she was playing that terrible day, but her body had been found, unidentified, exactly where she stated. Stephanie's murderer, to date, has not yet been apprehended.

After relaying her information to the ISPR team, Stephanie's demeanor changed for the better. She joined the other children as they played amongst the props and costumes in the attic and became very active during the Ghost

Expeditions that were conducted inside Le Petit Theatre. One afternoon, a Ghost Expedition group was ushered into Teddy's Corner. One of the participants, a man in his mid-forties, had already made quite a few enemies in the group by mocking the researcher at every property, and letting the group know that he knew better, for he was a *skeptic*. Inside the children's theatre, the group walked up to the stage and the skeptic walked off to the empty seats on the other side of the auditorium. The group was documenting drops in temperature while discussing how it physically felt like children were holding their hands. No one paid any further attention to the skeptic.

Back at the ISPR offices after the Ghost Expedition, each participant waited in line to receive their Completion Certificate—except the skeptic. He stood in the corner of the office as though he was looking at Dr. Montz's photos on the walls. Dr. Montz was in the office that day, and after everyone left, the skeptic turned around and said, "I only have one question for you. *IS* there a little girl ghost at that theatre named Stephanie?"

Dr. Montz looked at the skeptic, noting that it looked like the man had been crying, and told him about Stephanie. Dr. Montz explained that since Stephanie died so violently and recently, that it was too much for a lot of people, so the researchers were not to speak about her as an individual.

The skeptic said, "All I can say is that when I was sitting in that theatre, it felt like a little girl was sitting in my lap with her head against my chest. And all I could hear in my head, was "Stephanie, Stephanie..."

Le Petit Theatre main stage auditorium.

In addition to the other children entities, Stephanie was especially fond of an adult female entity at the theatre, Caroline.

Caroline is the most prevalently seen entity at Le Petit. Post-investigative research indicated that Caroline performed at the theatre from 1922 through 1924. At the young age of 22, she died one evening from an accidental fall from the attic balcony into the courtyard. Most entities will project an image of themselves of what they looked like shortly before they died. Interestingly enough, Caroline actually appears in different costumes. At times her long blonde hair is straight and loose and at other times, she is seen with elaborate, upswept hairstyles.

During one Ghost Expedition inside Le Petit Theatre, a young mother had her sleeping toddler in a stroller. While the researcher was pointing out the hot spots in the main auditorium, Caroline manifested herself upon the stage. The equipment began registering atmospheric changes as the toddler woke up and began speaking to Caroline. The little girl giggled when Caroline answered. This continued for almost ten minutes while the rest of the Ghost Expedition participants watched in awe. The little girl kept calling "Caroline, Pocahontas." Her mother explained later that *Pocahontas* was the child's favorite cartoon video. When it was time to depart, the little girl cried hysterically until the group exited through the main entrance back onto St. Peter Street. Once outside, the child immediately calmed down and fell back to sleep.

Caroline seemed to win the affection of all the workers at Le Petit. So often, while preparing new sets, the workers would place their tools down on the floor, only to turn around and find them gone. It was Caroline who they called aloud to, and many times, within moments, their tools were found again, right where they originally left them. Usually, the culprit behind the missing tools was the entity of a former Le Petit stagehand, Sigmund.

Sigmund began working at Le Petit in 1922. He worked for the theatre for many years and died in his 70s. Originally from Germany, Sigmund had a thick German accent to those who had audible experiences with him. He played mischievous pranks on the workers building new sets. He was fond of hiding their tools, disconnecting spotlights in the ceiling, altering music playing through the stereo system, and disrupting stage performances by closing curtains prematurely, turning the smoke machine on when it wasn't called for in the play, and gently pushing performers during their big moments on stage.

Dr. Montz first became familiar with Sigmund in 1990. Le Petit Theatre was one of his personal favorites for ongoing field reseach and throughout the years, he spent many long nights at the property. One evening, Dr. Montz was in the theatre late at night with two of the theatre directors. In the dark, the three men were in the balcony overlooking the main stage. They were listening to a great deal of unidentifible noise on the stage. The thought of rats crossed their minds as they ventured downstairs in the darkness of the auditorium to seek the answer. As they walked through the auditorium on the ground floor, the noise became louder, yet no easier to decipher. Very carefully, they climbed on stage. Dressed with a new set from an upcoming play, the stage

was chilly in temperature; much colder than anywhere else. The noise on stage seemed to move between the walls of the new set and traveled over the right side of the stage, over to a store room. The store room door was roughly sixteen feet high, tall enough to get the high walls of the sets and partial staircases inside. And now, the noise was coming from inside that room. Dr. Montz walked up to the huge wooden door, followed by the two theatre employees. He opened the door and was met with a wind—not a breeze, but a wind. In the darkness, Dr. Montz saw Sigmund for the first time. He could see Sigmund as an elderly man with salt and pepper hair, short. The entity then exited the room, first through the doorway and then continued on through Dr. Montz and the men behind him.

Sigmund proved to Dr. Montz and numerous documented witnesses that he was not a shy ghost.

In the years that followed, when Sigmund wanted to communicate with Dr. Montz, he usually manifested an apparition that Dr. Montz could see. Sigmund seemed to enjoy making people see his apparition. Sometimes, he liked to manifest just a partial image. On January 13, 1995, a late evening Ghost Expedition entered Le Petit Theatre from the back stage exit door on Chartres Street. The last person through the door was a young woman in her mid-twenties. The group almost hit the ceiling when halfway through the hallway, the woman in the back shrieked at the top of her lungs. Before the group could snap out of their state of shock and react to the screaming, the woman spun on her heels and ran screaming from the theatre back onto Chartres Street.

When she was calm enough to speak, she gave an interview. She explained that she was a little frightened about going into a haunted property. She was walking pretty close to her boyfriend in front of her, and all of a sudden, this arm and hand stretched out over her right shoulder. She thought someone wanted to pass her in the hallway. She looked down at the hand, looked behind her to see who it was, but there was no one. She whipped her neck back to see the arm and hand but they were gone. That's when she found her lungs and legs.

In 1992, a young woman was employed at Le Petit Theatre as receptionist and box office manager. The box office is located in the foyer, closer to the children's theatre. One night, the woman's boyfriend arrived at the theatre to take her home. She still had an hour's worth of work to complete, so she told her boyfriend to sit anywhere he felt comfortable and wait. The boyfriend had never been in the theatre after-hours and decided to take himself on a little tour. When he walked into the main auditorium, he saw an elderly gentleman moving some tools on the stage. The man turned around and waved at the boyfriend and motioned for him to sit down. The boyfriend sat down and was joined by the elderly man who introduced himself as Sigmund. For the next twenty minutes, the boyfriend listened to Sigmund's entertaining tales of per-

Opposite page: Cement stairwell leading to the Le Petit Theatre attic.

formances, different sets and some of the colorful actors that performed on the stage. The boyfriend was taken with the colorful stories and invited Sigmund to join him and his girlfriend for dinner. Sigmund accepted the invitation.

When the receptionist was finished with her work for the evening, she went looking for her boyfriend. Not seeing him in the foyer or lobby, she walked into the main auditorium. In the middle of the center section, she saw her boyfriend laughing. She called his name and he stood up and turned around. He called to her across the auditorium and informed her that he invited Sigmund for dinner but as he glanced back to his conversation mate, the chair was empty. Sigmund was no longer in sight.

Sigmund was not the only entity that enjoyed the main auditorium. His love of the theatre was matched by that of Aljandro Venegas. Aljandro was a Spaniard, with very tall, sharp facial features, thick black hair, and a mustache. He appeared to those who saw him in formal wear from the early 1800s. Aljandro was most often seen in the balcony section of the main auditorium. Looking up at the balcony, one can see his favorite seat: front row, second seat in from the aisle to the left that separated the end and middle sections. While the main auditorium was empty of patrons, it was not uncommon to hear Aljandro's seat flip down.

Aljandro was non-intrusive in the backstage activities at the theatre. He did, however, make his presence known during many performances. At times, patrons with a ticket matching Aljandro's seat would travel up to the balcony to be seated for the performance, only to find a man in strange formal wear already seated. Aljandro always refused to move to another seat, which resulted in the patron making his or her way back downstairs to the box office to complain. The patrons were always told that the *gentleman in formal attire* has moved seats. And sure enough, each patron would return and find the seat empty.

During many Ghost Expeditions, the researcher would usher the participants on the main auditorium stage and have them stand on the side closest to the open attic above them. At times, someone in the group would break down and cry before two minutes elapsed. That's how the researcher knew that Katherine was close at hand.

Katherine was an aspiring actress who died in 1926. She committed suicide in the theatre after being turned down for a promised part in an upcoming production. While standing at the edge of the open attic, overlooking the stage, she tied one of the weighted ropes around her neck and jumped off. When Katherine manifests herself, she appears with long black hair and wears a bright yellow dress. People empathically experience her overwhelming sense of despair while standing on the stage if Katherine is present. Reactions included crying and difficulty in breathing. When Katherine was not present on the side of the stage, she was often found crying upstairs in an attic corner, surrounded by colorful costumes.

Katherine shares the attic with a negative entity, Perry. It is believed that Perry was a slave in New Orleans during the Spanish Governor's rule. He appears very large, threatening and produces a foul odor. Foul odors are quite common with negative entities. Most patrons have never encountered Perry, but he has made himself known to many theatre workers and of course, the ISPR Team. One night, Perry gave a performance that the witnesses will never forget.

In mid August of 1995, Dr. Montz was having dinner with one investigator, two Ghost Expedition researchers, a journalist from Canada, and a published magazine photographer. Before dessert arrived, Dr. Montz answered a page that originated from Le Petit Theatre. He asked his group if they would like to accompany him around the corner to the theatre while he spoke with the theatre manager about an urgent issue. ISPR's work in Le Petit was no secret to this group and they all jumped at the chance to enter the theatre afterhours. Dr. Montz and his party walked up to the side stage exit on Chartres Street, where the manager was waiting. He took Dr. Montz aside briefly while the rest of the group waited eagerly to get inside. Dr. Montz was first through the door, followed by the manager, the investigator and researchers, the journalist, and the photographer. The door slammed behind the photographer after she crossed the threshold. Startled by the sudden bang of the door, the photographer, with her camera around her neck, took two giant steps and hooked her arm through the journalist's to walk right by her side. Once the group made it to the backstage area (technically to the side of the main stage), the photographer tried to snap off a few shots—but her camera refused to work. The manager turned on a light and the photographer was shocked to see that her brand-new battery had drained to zero. As though sharing that information with the group was a cue, the light overhead began to get dimmer. The atmosphere felt heavier, and without warning, the journalist began to cry hysterically. As Dr. Montz tried to get the journalist to sit down on a chair, the photographer let out a small scream and ripped her camera by the neckband off her neck and placed it on the ground. The camera was too hot to the touch. Everyone substantiated this by burning their fingers, one person at a time. The journalist continued to wail.

The manager had moved through the doorway facing the courtyard, where the stairwell to the attic stands to the right. The photographer volunteered to stay with the journalist while the rest of the group made its way upstairs. Dr. Montz led the manager halfway up the steps, where they both came to an abrupt halt. The investigator and one researcher were just two steps behind while the other researcher was closer to the bottom of the steps. Something dark was blocking the way. The electrical charge in the air was incredible and fear washed over the last three people on the steps. The investigator and researcher turned around to check on the last researcher just in time to see a very large, shirtless, black man standing behind him. The researcher sensed the shock from the other two and turned around and saw the man, just two steps away from him. The researcher screamed and without hesitation ran back through the doorway to the journalist and photographer. The investigator and researcher stayed—better to stick with Dr. Montz then to follow the others. Within a minute, the remaining party of four on the steps heard the back stage exit door slam.

Corner of clothing aisle of Le Petit Theatre where
the entity of Katherine is often found crying.

Aisle of props in Le Petit Theatre attic.

The darkness blocking the steps dissipated. Dr. Montz and the manager climbed the second set of stairs up to the locked attic door. The key would not unlock the door. Dr. Montz took his turn at the key and sternly requested to be let in, and the key worked without a problem. The small group entered the wing of the attic that stores the racks and racks of costumes. Audible crying was heard from the back corner. In the area where the wings intersect, there stood the large male entity that was seen on the stairs, the slave, Perry. He was yelling in anger at the group while shaking his fist in a threatening manner. Perry's temper was not heard audibly, but the intense negative energy was overwhelmning. To this day, Dr. Montz regrets that he did not have any of his equipment with him that night.

Perry continued to scream for minutes while the group stood and watched, motionless. Finally, Dr. Montz held up his hand as one would do to reassure a child and said in a calming voice, "alright." Perry faded away. Abruptly, the crying ceased.

It appeared that Perry and Katherine had put an early end to the set construction that night.

The ISPR has always maintained that entities have the ability to travel wherever they choose. This theory was originally substantiated in New Orleans by the ISPR during the first investigation of another property in the French Quarter. During the initial investigation of Crescent City Books, the ISPR Team found the children of Le Petit Theatre.

Police sketch artist Renee Spar draws her impression of
Katherine hiding in the attic of Le Petit Theatre.

Inside Teddy's Corner, the children's theatre.

View of Teddy's Corner from Jackson Square.

–Little Girl in the Haunted Slave Quarter–
St. Peter Street

When Parapsychologist Dr. Larry Montz began his six-year paranormal research study for the ISPR in 1990, he actually moved into a haunted slave quarter apartment building. The following is an excerpt from his journal notes.

I was asked to investigate the slave quarter by the current resident because of the apparitions seen here and the poltergeist activity that takes place quite often. She stated that occasionally, a chair, vase, or candlestick holders are physically moved, and a white cloud has been seen in one of the bedrooms upstairs. She has had many chilling experiences of the paranormal here, and also happened to have a spare bedroom for rent. I decided to rent the second bedroom and live amongst the spirits of the past. I've investigated many haunted places, but never had the chance to spend more than a couple of days in a house. I had to find out more about this little spirit and the other entities that walk these premises.

The activity in this house can definitely make a skeptic into a believer. Even without my equipment, I could tell immediately that this was an actively haunted property. This deteriorating structure, tormented by time, stands behind an old house in the 900 block of St. Peter Street in the French Quarter, between Dauphine and Burgundy Streets.

Built in 1824, this slave quarter follows the classic design of many houses built during this period. In the French Quarter, the houses were built with the main house near the street, and another detached, one- or two-story structure in the rear. The two properties were usually separated by a colorful courtyard overflowing with trees and foliage, surrounded by high brick walls and antique brick flooring. This rear building served as the kitchen and living quarters for the slaves or hired help. Today, the main house has been converted into a duplex and the slave quarter is a two-bedroom apartment. The slave quarter has six french doors, constructed mostly of glass. Massive dark green wooden doors from the original structure are used to cover all of the inner glass doors. A gallery, the 1800s term for balcony, lined with wooden railings, travels along the entire front of the building separating the first floor from the second.

I entered the wooden gate next to the main house and walked along the old brick path to the courtyard between the slave quarter and the main house. There was a damp and moldy feeling, the energy here was indeed peculiar. I could sense a dark feeling of sadness, turmoil, and death in several areas.

While I was standing in the center of the courtyard, I felt an overwhelming sensation of people watching me, standing around me, and wanting to touch me. Was this just energy from the past?

Rumor has it that this property was once an unmarked burial ground for epidemic victims. The original French Quarter boundaries stopped at Dauphine Street. North of Dauphine was an old ditch, and past that, a cemetery. In those days, people were buried in cemeteries according to social status, religion or heritage. During the epidemics, bodies were buried wherever space was available. This could explain why the energy was so intense and complex here and why there's so much paranormal activity in the courtyard and slave quarter.

When I approached the entrance door of the slave quarter, the energy changed—it was very intense. My heart started racing. Chills raced through my body and goose bumps felt like ants crawling over my skin in a frenzy. This house was haunted. The presence of a child was unmistakable. A very active little spirit was playing in the house when I entered. I immediately got an image of a light-skinned girl with long, dark hair, about ten years of age.

As I walked toward the stairs, I could feel her presence so strongly that I automatically said, "Hi! Just came to visit, hope you don't mind." I almost expected to trip over one of her invisible toys on the floor. She seemed to be sitting on the stairs, her face peeking between the railings. I couldn't see her, but she was there; it felt like I could have touched her, she was so real. When I approached her, she moved up the stairs as if she wanted me to follow. She didn't seem to be frightened but was rather happy about a new visitor. Apparently this house is where she often plays, and I didn't get the feeling that she actually lived here, but was possibly watched over here at times. When I reached the second step, her presence faded away. My heart and pulse returned to normal.

I then examined the objects that were reported to have moved. The energy around the vase was so strong I expected to see little fingerprints on the dark burgundy glass of the antique vase. The chair moves from a brick wall over to the front of the french doors, about three feet. This little girl definitely haunts this house, but she's not alone. I was excited about moving in.

After I moved in to my new slave quarter apartment, I spent a couple of days cleaning and setting up my part of the house. The mud and sod bricks that make up the walls are so old and the sand mortar between them disintegrates daily. The building is actually sinking into the ground; there's always a damp, musty feeling in the house. The french doors and windows no longer fit snug to the bricks and there are gaps between them while the solid outside green doors partially hang on their old rusted hinges. I decided to seal the gaps to keep the air-conditioning in; the temperature upstairs was at least ten degrees warmer than downstairs. I was standing on the ladder, reaching for the top of the window, and suddenly a cold chill came over me as my heart started to race. Then I heard someone ask, "What are you doing?" The voice was so clear that I automatically replied, "I'm just sealing up the cracks to keep it cooler in here." I could feel the presence of the little girl again. She had

Haunted slave quarter apartment building. Dr. Montz occupied a second-floor bedroom in this building.

come in the house, up the stairs, and was standing behind me. I guess she was just curious, for after I replied her presence disappeared.

Later that same day, I was outside on the gallery sealing the doors on the right corner of my bedroom. The atmosphere felt heavy, especially at this end of the gallery. I finished and went back into my room. As I was leaving my room, out of the corner of my eye, there were *three* little faces pressed up against the glass doors. They were staring right at me from the gallery. It was the little girl I had encountered earlier, with a younger, smaller boy and another little girl. When I turned back toward them, the faces disappeared. My research project has kicked off to a great start!

One day, I arrived home at dusk. I experienced a strong feeling as I walked through the courtyard, a much different feeling then the first day. I retrieved my mail and sat in my living room to open it. My cat caught my attention as she took off for the main entry door. I thought it was a visitor. I went to the doors but no one was there. The cat stayed focused in an attack stance. As I passed back through the living room, I saw a dark figure standing outside in the courtyard near the front door. There were no clear facial features, just the form of a tall man. I watched this figure float from door to door, as my cat trailed behind him. The event was timed at just under two minutes. Fantastic.

During my four-month residency, this event with the shadow man took place twice more. The little girl and her friends were very active. I saw several apparitions, especially the little girl's blue dress on a number occasions. I could see her dress so clearly; it was a party dress with lace and ruffles. At times, I experienced audible phenomenon—hearing her dress rustle as she walked or ran. The woman who lived there also reported that she also saw the little girl quite often, watching and hearing her run up the stairs. Over the first few months, they communicated telepathically their names and ages: Katherine is eight, the boy is her brother Josh, six years of age. The other girl was about ten or twelve, but she would not relate her name. I tested several clairvoyants at the property. The entities communicated the same information to each clairvoyant.

At times, the kids still use their "playhouse," running up and down the old wooden stairs and out onto the balcony overlooking the courtyard. All clairvoyant determinations said that they were alive between 1845 and 1855, and probably died of yellow fever. In checking the historical records, I found that the first yellow fever epidemic was in 1793, the last in 1905. The epidemic, however, that killed the highest number of people in New Orleans was suffered in 1853.

The clairvoyants all sensed pretty much the same series of events. They saw that the siblings' mother was deathly ill. The children were sent outside to play with the little girl from the slave quarter. While outside, the mother died. Today, Katherine still moves the chair, sits on it and waits for her mom to take her and her brother home.

For the sake of the children, Dr. Montz had the property cleared shortly before moving out.

Maxwell's Jazz Cabaret
615 Toulouse Street

One of the leading authentic jazz clubs in New Orleans, up until 1998, was Maxwell's Jazz Cabaret. Although it was not considered an historical property by the city of New Orleans, it became known throughout the city as Harry Connick, Sr.'s favorite club in which to perform, and garnered international publicity through the ISPR for its haunting activities.

The first ISPR Investigation of Maxwell's Jazz Cabaret was conducted on February 6, 1996. The ISPR was contacted by Jimmy Maxwell, the club's owner. He had reports of a vast array of disturbances, although he himself had never had any experiences. Employees complained that items left on one table would disappear and reappear on different tables. They would see shadows gliding across the stage between performances, as did many patrons. Loud bangs and scraping sounds of equipment being dragged across the stage behind the closed curtains were heard by management and other employees when

Maxwell's Toulouse Cabaret was a favorite haunt of Harry Connick, Sr.

the stage was completely empty. Strange sensations, including intense cold-ness and body chills, were reported by employees and patrons alike. At first, employees tried to convince themselves as well as their guests, that it was just the air conditioning, but they knew that it felt differently.

The architecture of the club, as it stood in the early and mid-1990s, was a plain and classic design. When one entered from Toulouse Street, there was a bar to the left as well as tables throughout the lobby. To enter the cabaret room, one had to walk up a few steps and pass through a glass door. There were tables and chairs descending down to the stage on three levels of plat-forms. When the stage curtain was drawn, it was red to match the tablecloths; everything else was a flat black. The stage was a hotbed of paranormal activ-ity, as was the right-hand wall, closest to the Mississippi River. There was a black exit door in this wall on the ground floor. Behind this door was a narrow hallway, leading nowhere, and one could not see it from the front of the build-ing on Toulouse Street. Many Ghost Expedition participants received images of secret liasons taking place in this private hallway while Mardi Gras rowdiness and merriment took place at a dizzying rate outside. Above the black exit door is an exposed wooden staircase, painted black, that led to a narrow balcony seating area, large enough for three deuces, one behind the other. This bal-cony could also access the catwalk that went completely behind the public area walls at the back of the cabaret room, and riverside wall of the outer lobby. At this point, there was a door which allowed one to continue on a catwalk around the front of the bar/lobby area and back through another door, which leads to the administrative offices behind the second-story wall, the side of Maxwell's close to the former Ghost Expedition Office, just a few doors away toward Royal Street.

During the first investigation by the ISPR, the team documented several cold spots and located different areas where there were very unusual electro-magnetic energy field readings. Over the years, we have documented that a presence has the ability to create an unusually high electro-magnetic field, measured commonly by a magnetometer. This is generally in the same area where a clairvoyant or clairsentient investigator feels or sees a presence. Dr. Montz's notes recap the first investigation.

The team and I have found two entities present. Both were affiliated with this property during the 1920s. The first entity is a heavy-set black male wearing a white shirt, suspenders, black pants and several gold rings with gemstones. He was a band member, actually a trumpet player. He was between 40 and 50 years old. Julia was the first to see him standing on the stage next to the piano. He did try to communicate, and Julia was able to get his name, Arthur. He was a gambler and quite often owed large sums of money to "bankers." He died of a heart attack; overweight and under tremendous stress. Daena saw him as a shadow.

The second entity is a white male, early 20s, Italian. He has black hair is worn slicked back. He is of average height and weight with no other distin-guishing features. He wears a tuxedo and appears to be the man that after

Maxwell's Toulouse Jazz Cabaret

Catwalk in Maxwell's outer lobby bar.

checked people at the door of this private club. We got the impression that he had been trying to persuade a woman he loved to return his affections and leave her husband. That was a little sketchy—it appears that the husband was "connected," could have been a boss, and had our doorman killed. All the past images we got of this place definitely points to the mafia— the private club, the decor, the heavy cigarette smoke, the secretive air.

As I was recording EM readings by the stairs that lead down to the main floor, the meters jumped and a very cold breeze hit my face. At the same time, Mike turned to me and described the entity in the tuxedo. The entity tried to lead Mike to the right rear corner of the theater, where the bathroom is located. This is the same area where I saw a past image of a door that existed in the 1870 building. When Mike saw it later; he described the same image to me.

After leading us in that direction, he stopped and stood still. The EM reading stayed constant for 4.5 minutes, until the entity turned and walked through the right side wall. The EM readings then returned to normal for that area.

Second past image received of a man in a tuxedo opening the door and another man in a dark suit, overcoat and hat, standing in the alleyway, pulling a revolver and shooting the man at the door. We think this is the young man that now haunts Maxwell's. The gunman was one of the Mafia's hit men.

Usually, the investigation is concluded and we return only if requested by the client. In this very unique situation, because Ghost Expeditions will be entering this site daily, new data may be compiled. Many of the Ghost Expedition participants are certain to have experiences inside the theater.

Post-investigation research found historical records that indicated that there was no house ever standing at this location until 1746. In that year, a new brick house, warehouse, and kitchen were built by Louis Wiltz after he swapped two other lots on St. Louis Street in exchange for this property. There were no changes until 1789 and 1793; at both points there is a mention of the "lot" being surveyed by the Louisiana State University Archives Department. The

1746 building burned in the 1788 fire that swept through the French Quarter, and the lot stood vacant until 1795 when a new building was constructed. No other buildings are mentioned in the records until 1810 when the property was sold again "with existing buildings."

Sixty years went by before another entry was made in the property records. In 1870, the buildings were torn down and new brick structures were erected— a three-story brick store with ground floor cast-iron columns; a two-story brick rear building; water closets, and cistern. Then, from 1909 to 1927, this property was listed as a veterinary hospital owned by Vincent Li Rocchi. It is believed that during this time, the front lobby of Maxwell's was used as the vet's office, but it was a front for the private club in the cabaret room.

Entrance to cabaret

In the late 1920s, a two-story brick automobile repair shop was built, utilizing the rear walls of the 1870 structure. The building served as the Civil Sheriff's repair garage. The building stood unchanged until the late 1960s, at which time it was razed and replaced by the current building, constructed in 1970. The rear wall and sections of the side walls still remain from the older structure that dates back to 1870.

After the initial ISPR Investigation of Maxwell's Jazz Cabaret, it was placed on the Ghost Expedition site list. Dr. Montz's predictions were correct—many, many participants had paranormal experiences in the theater or cabaret room. So many, in fact, that Maxwell's was elevated to an advanced level Ghost Expedition site. Advanced Ghost Expeditions were conducted late in the night, after the property closed for business. These Ghost Expeditions always attract a lot of clairvoyant people who want to know more about their abilities and the ISPR's progressive means of paranormal field research. As a result, Ghost Expeditions collected so much more information for study by the ISPR. The subjective information first documented by Dr. Montz was revised as more information became clear.

It was not the wife of another man that the tuxedoed man pursued. She was the daughter of the mafia boss for whom the tuxedoed man worked. It was the mafia boss who had the young man killed, in the club. He was shot in the back while he climbed the side stairs to the narrow balcony/exit. The ISPR continued to collect more in-depth information. Shortly, the ISPR had enough subjective information to piece together the theory that the tuxedoed man was running alcohol from Iowa through Chicago and Kansas City down to New Orleans, and skimming some profit off his shipments. That was the reason he was murdered by his potential future father-in-law. This theory makes the most sense and the logistics of the theory were substantiated by several weeks of research by phone and internet. The romantic connections between the man and the mafia boss' daughter was substantiated by the daughter's entity, Anna Maria, in January of 1997. It was almost a year since the first ISPR Investigation was conducted, and almost a year of daily Ghost Expeditions. The new ISPR Investigation was conducted with different clairvoyants and two of the original investigators, and was re-

corded professionally by a production company.

Anna Maria, the love interest of the tuxedoed man, daughter of the mafia boss who ordered his death, spoke for two separate sessions, all documented on camera. By the time of this investigation, Dr. Montz already knew that Anna Maria existed and that she always appeared in white with dark hair falling in banana curls down to her waist. She had been described over and over as looking "angelic." In association with Anna Maria's presence was the rich smell of white roses, and she used one of the investigators to communicate. The following is a published article written by one of the production companies' executive producers, Jack Roth. Jack's article was published in the former *Hauntings Today* newsletter, and the ISPR appreciated and enjoyed the wonderful and unsolicited testimony.

On January 16, 1997, I arrive in New Orleans feeling a bit apprehensive. The thought of documenting footage of Dr. Larry Montz and his team investigating haunted properties excited me, but it was also a little unnerving. Yes, the footage would serve as part of a pilot episode for a new television series based on paranormal phenomena. And yes, I suppose that for the sake of good drama I wanted something to happen. But what happened at Maxwell's Jazz Cabaret exceeded my wildest expectations, and it will remain etched in my memory forever.

From this day forward people will ask me to describe what I experienced.

At first I truly believed I could never accurately convey such an experience. I soon realized, however, that it would be easy for me to describe what happened at Maxwell's. It's part of the oldest and most endearing story ever told. Quite simply, it's a love story.

Dr. Montz's investigative team consisted of five people that day,

Maxwell's outer lobby bar.

Maxwell's lobby bar.

including Dr. Montz, his assistant Ed, and clairovyant investigators Jillian, Daena, and Maria. Maria has incredible channeling abilities. Channeling consists of having an entity take over your body for a brief period of time. For the purposes of paranormal investigations, it provides an important communication link to entities. Often, the information provided through channeling is essential to subsequent research.

Maxwell's is not new to Dr. Montz and his team. In fact, all three psychics have felt the presence of several entities there at one time or another during previous investigations. One entity in particular, however, seemed special to me. Her name is Anna Maria. In life, she was a striking young girl with angelic beauty who frequented Maxwell's when it was a speakeasy in the 1920s. The love of her life, an Italian gangster who owned the club, also apparently roams the premises. From the information Dr. Montz and his team have been able to gather, it appears that Anna Maria's father was also a gangster. He was adamantly against his 18-year-old daughter seeing this man, so he had him killed. Anna Maria, devestated by his death, died of a broken heart shortly thereafter.

This sounds like a great story, but I wasn't convinced. As a producer, I need to be open-minded, but I also need to be rational. I required tangible evidence in order to make a reasonable assertion. I entered the old establishment with a cautious attitude.

Once inside, Maria felt a strong psychic impression of Anna Maria. She described, from past experiences, how Anna Maria was associated with the scent of white roses. She also told us how Anna Maria would always sit with her Italian love at a balcony table. I glanced up at the balcony and imagined what it must have been like for this young couple to share a once-in-a-lifetime bond during one of the happiest times in American history. If, in fact, they can't leave Maxwell's because of the memories they shared there in life, I can sincerely understand why. The tragic ending to this story, whether true or not, ripped through my heart and made me very, very sad.

When we reached the stage, Maria started to shake violently. She told Dr. Montz that Anna Maria was present. Dr. Montz, in an attempt to gather more information, asked Maria if she would try to channel Anna Maria. She agreed, and what happened next could truly be labeled extraordinary. Suddenly, with the stage lights dancing on her face, Maria changed. Her features softened and her eyes seemed to grow larger. She looked up at Dr. Montz solemnly. She had become beauty in its purest form.

After several questions, Dr. Montz asked Anna Maria what was the name of her love.

"Nicole (pronounced Neeko)," Maria replied in an Italian accent. "Are there other people here with you?" Dr. Montz asked. "There's only Nicole," she said. "Would you like to leave this place with Nicole?" Dr. Montz asked. "No. These were the best times. Everybody was so happy. Unfinished business," she said.

I was mesmerized. Either Maria was the best actress since Meryl Streep or we were witnessing something astonishing. Dr. Montz continued his questioning, and I continued to stare at Maria's face, or was it Anna Maria's face?

Suddenly, Maria looked up past Dr. Montz to the balcony. Her eyes longing, she stared at the balcony as if she could see her soul mate in human form for the first time in seventy years through Maria's eyes.

"Is Nicole up there?" Dr. Montz asked. She nodded her head as tears welled up in her eyes. "He's so beautiful. I miss him so much," she said. At this moment, I was completely convinced that I had just witnessed something phenomenal. I felt a heavy sadness as I realized my eyes had filled with tears, as well.

Dr. Montz finished his questioning and asked Anna Maria to leave Maria's body. She agreed, but only after looking up at the balcony for a few moments more. And as suddenly as it had begun, it was over. Maria was back, wondering why we were all looking at her in utter amazement.

As we left the stage, I noticed Maria smelling her hands. She had a smile on her face and looked as if she were very much at peace. I asked her what she was doing, and she told me that she could smell the white roses all over her body. I leaned towards her and smelled her neck. White roses, so beautiful and fragrant. I'll never forget the smell, as real as anything my senses have ever registered.

We're planning on returning to Maxwell's one day. We must. We owe it to Anna Maria and Nicole to share their story with the rest of the world. They say that love never dies...I know this now to be the truth.

The ISPR is known for its progressive applications of Psi abilities in field research, the most exciting aspect of parapsychology to the ISPR Investigators. While accomplishing successful investigations to achieve one goal, Dr. Montz is able to study various clairvoyant abilities outside of the lab. The ability exercised by Maria, when channeling Anna Maria, was mediumship. Maria was a non-cognizant medium. This kind of ability can be extremely dangerous.

The ISPR featured Maxwell's on a variety of television shows and, until the ISPR closed its New Orleans branch, it studied the paranormal activities of Maxwell's on a daily basis. It was noted for almost two years that the cocktail waitresses were uncomfortable about spending time by themselves inside the cabaret. And several times during that period, employees had opened the cabaret in the morning to find one candle burning on a front middle table, closest to the stage. This was especially interesting, for even if an employee had left a candle burning overnight, the time frame between closing and opening could be eight to twelve hours, depending on tourist traffic, and the candles were only four-hour votives. Through Ghost Expeditions the ISPR conducted empathic testing at Maxwell's similar to that which was applied at Le Petit Theatre. As so many participants felt Katherine's influence on stage at Le Petit Theatre, almost half that number *experienced* the musician's heart attack on stage as well as a gun shot on the wooden stairs above the side exit door. Maxwell's Jazz Cabaret was consistently a favorite Ghost Expedition site.

Napoleon House Restaurant
500 Chartres Street

The Napoleon House restaurant opened for business in 1914. The sign over the door boasts an establishment date of 1797. However, the original house was actually constructed as a residence in 1814 by New Orleans Mayor Girod (the date is provided on the plaque with the official Orleans Parish seal on the side of the building). In 1821, while at a party, Mayor Girod offered his house to Napoleon should he decide to take refuge in the United States. Although Napoleon never set foot on American soil, the house was named for him.

The ISPR has conducted several informal investigations of the property between 1990 and 1996. Two entities actively haunt the property.

The first entity is a female and appears to have been a Mammy. Almost three decades of professional paranormal research has revealed to the ISPR that many entities stay earthbound, but not always because of revenge or that they are *trapped*, but because they are watching family members or a particular property. The Mammy that haunts the Napoleon House was most often

The Napoleon House, before renovations, viewed from third-floor courtroom during an ISPR investigation of the French Quarter Courthouse.

Napoleon House Restaurant.

seen in the courtyard of the building. In the mid-1990s, the Napoleon House Restaurant underwent a total facelift. Quite often, during restoration or renovations of actively haunted properties, the paranormal phenomena increases. It's usually due to the entity being upset by the construction and/or turmoil. The Mammy was no exception. During the time of restoration, the energy inside the restaurant was heavier and oppressive. Several times, during the renovations, bartenders would document that a bottle behind the bar would topple over for no apparent reason at all. After the construction work was complete, the Mammy was seen again outside in the courtyard and the atmosphere inside the building returned to its original light feel again.

The Napoleon House is on the corner of Chartres and St. Louis Streets. While standing on St. Louis, one can sometimes get a glimpse of the upstairs guest rooms above the Napoleon House. Beautifully appointed with period decor, the guest rooms and outside balcony staircase are home to many sightings of a civil war soldier. The entity has never been friendly nor communicative during ISPR investigations, but his presence is difficult to miss. Often appearing solid, he disappears around a corner quickly when realizing he is being seen. The most common experience noted with this entity is difficulty in breathing.

New Orleans Pharmacy Museum
514 Chartres Street

This historic apothecary shop was built in 1823 and operated by Dr. Duffulo, one of the first registered pharmacists in the United States. In 1857, the pharmacy was purchased by a French pharmacist, Dr. Dupas. Within these walls, Dupas imposed shocking experiments on pregnant slaves. He died in 1867 from complications of syphilis. The Pharmacy Museum is owned by the city and the employees have been ordered not to speak about the entities at the property and its hauntings.

Inside, the Pharmacy Museum houses blood-drawing instruments, 19th century drugs, and a soda fountain that dates back to 1855. It is also home to the negative entity of Dr. Dupas. Dupas is often seen standing on the ground floor of the museum after hours. He wears a brown suit; sometimes with a white lab coat. He appears to be about sixty-five years of age, short and stocky, and sports a dark mustache. Dupas is responsible for setting off the museum's alarm systems, moving items in locked display cases, and throwing books in the meeting room on the second floor.

One night in August of 1993, Dr. Montz was about to conduct another investigation of the Pharmacy Museum after a museum worker complained that an unseen force pushed her on the staircase leading to the second-floor meeting room. Dr. Montz was standing outside the front entrance of the museum, waiting for the employee to arrive with the keys. As the employee walked up to Dr. Montz, the alarm inside was set off. When they entered the building and cut the alarm, they found that the alarm was a sound detector, triggered by a sound like breaking glass. The alarm system printout confirmed that, but no one was inside. No glass was broken—in fact, nothing had been disturbed.

In the case of a negative entity such as Dupas, some sensitive people will experience empathic physical reactions. Merely standing outside of the Pharmacy Museum when Dupas is present, the ISPR has documented hundreds who have experienced shortness of breath, nausea and various body pains. Women, especially pregnant women, were documented to be the most susceptible.

In the carriageway beside the Pharmacy Museum that leads from Chartres Street to the courtyard, several clairvoyants have received two impressions. The first is of bodies being lowered from the second floor (where Dupas conducted his hideous experiments), into a waiting carriage. Trap doors were discovered during an ISPR investigation of the pharmacy, where not only bodies could have been lowered, but where supplies were lifted and brought into the building. The other frequent impression is received behind the Pharmacy Museum, in the courtyard.

In the courtyard, there is a site where two slave quarter buildings used to stand. Slave quarter buildings were traditionally very small and could house up to twenty people at a time. Ghost Expeditions used this area as a continuous Psi experiment. Without providing any information, the Ghost Expedition researcher would have each person stand in a designated area, and would ask them to relate any impressions or physical feelings they may experience. Many volunteers claimed to experience great sensations of claustrophobia. After the documentation was completed for each experiment, it was then revealed to each group what kind of building stood here in years gone by.

Further back in the courtyard, an apparition of a young woman sitting by the fountain, wearing a large chapeau with a feather, was documented over a three-year period. From information garnered in a clairvoyant manner, this apparition has no connection with the Pharmacy Museum but is related to the buildings on the opposite side of the fountain.

The optimum time to visit the Pharmacy Museum for an increased opportunity to experience Dr. Dupas is after hours. If Dupas is present, one's chance of seeing objects move, or Dr. Dupas himself, increase dramatically. ISPR statistics from New Orleans Ghost Expeditions over a three-year period indicate a frequency of experiencing paranormal phenomenon at the site at about 40 percent.

Dr. Dupas still haunts the New Orleans Pharmacy Museum.

The carriageway, under the 516 address, leads to the courtyard behind the Pharmacy Museum where slave quarter buildings once stood. Many clairvoyant impressions of bodies being lowered into the carriageway have been noted.

O'Flaherty's Irish Channel Pub

514 Toulouse Street

The first of the two buildings that are now O'Flaherty's Irish Channel Pub, was constructed in 1798, the second, several years later. Originally, the buildings contained businesses downstairs and living quarters on the upper floors. Throughout the devastating epidemics that ravaged the French Quarter, the second floor at this property was utilized as a quarantine house for those afflicted and waiting to die. In 1853 alone, over 11,000 French Quarter residents died from an epidemic of yellow fever.

When the current owner, Danny O'Flaherty bought the property, he was the first to note the paranormal activity within the buildings and courtyard. When he contacted the ISPR, he had three questions that needed to be answered. Who was the woman in the balcony, why were his employees so frightened, and why were there old security bars on the third-floor windows?

During the first ISPR Investigation of O'Flaherty's Irish Channel Pub, Dr. Montz ushered his team into the courtyard first. The clairvoyant investigators immediately picked up on negative energy right under the third-floor window and on the the raised patio at the other end of the courtyard. While examining the patio, one of the clairvoyants turned around to look at the third-floor windows again, and saw an image of a man hanging from one end of a rope; the other end was inside the third floor window. Clairvoyantly, the investigators felt residual energy from a woman on the balcony in the Ballad Room. During that investigation, the three clairvoyant investigators refused to travel to the third floor. Dr. Montz and an assistant found several high electro-magnetic fields throughout the empty third floor, not generated by anything natural.

During the following investigations, more subjective information was received. Clairvoyantly, the name of Mary Ellen was received over and over. They also received information on an affair, a murder, and then, a suicide. After the post-investigative research was conducted using the files in the Historic New Orleans Collection, the pieces of the puzzle fell into place and made sense.

In 1806, 24-year-old Mary Wheaton, from Cumberland, New Jersey, married Joseph Bapentier, the third and then-current owner of the buildings. Bapentier owned a general feed store and he and his new wife lived on the second floor, over what is now the Ballad Room. In 1810, Bapentier murdered his mistress, a young French woman named Angelique.

Bapentier and Angelique were engaged in a terrible argument on the patio of the courtyard. Angelique ran from Bapentier, through the courtyard into the general feed store and up two flights of steps to the third floor. Bapentier chased her onto the third floor and through to the front of the building which faces Toulouse. Bapentier grabbed Angelique by the neck and began to throttle her. As he choked his victim, he dragged her back to the back side of the third floor, overlooking the courtyard, and threw her from the window (the second window from the right when facing the two buildings in the courtyard). Angelique smashed into the ground, head first, and broke her neck.

When Bapentier threw Angelique to her death, he was not aware of the little black boy who was sitting above him on the fourth-floor windowsill and

Behind the third floor window, epidemic victims were kept prisoner until their deaths. Joseph Bapentier is sometimes viewed hanging by his neck from the same window.

saw Angelique go flying out of the window to die on the ground below. Bapentier ran to the courtyard and heard a gasp. He looked up and saw the young witness. Bapentier was frightened for himself. He dragged Angelique's body over to the elevated patio where a sewage well then existed. He threw her body into the well to dispose of it. At this point, Bapentier heard the young boy scream and saw him run off from the window, probably to get help. Bapentier didn't waste any time; he knew he was in trouble. He ran back into the build-

Ghost Expedition participants often saw Mary standing in this second floor window. She was consistantly described with shoulder-length black hair and a white dress.

Poltergeist activity was common in the Celtic gift store; usually in the form of books thrown to the middle of the floor from the bookcases.

ing, up to the third floor, tied a noose out of rope, and threw himself to his death by hanging.

As a result of Bapentier's death, Mary Wheaton inherited the buildings and resided there until 1817. At age 35, she fell ill and died. With no heirs to the property, the records indicate it was soon auctioned off.

O'Flaherty's Irish Channel Pub provided a hotbed of documented paranormal phenomena during ISPR Investigations and ISPR's Ghost Expeditions throughout the early and mid-1990s. Mary was often seen from the courtyard staring out of the second floor window over the staircase, adjacent to the Ballad Room. It was common for guests, during performances in the Ballad Room, to see her sitting alone in the balcony. Many guests inquired about sitting up in the balcony, too. When they were told that the balcony was closed to patrons, they would insist that they saw a woman sitting there. O'Flaherty' s Irish Channel Pub employees soon learned to tell these patrons that the woman they saw was an exception, for she lived on the property.

Even new employees had frequent encounters with Mary. She was very protective of the property, and if she felt that a certain employee was not up to par, she made her presence known, and not in a friendly manner—by pushing, tripping, and tapping on shoulders. If the employee didn't shape up, they certainly didn't last too long. The owner was so fond of Mary, that he named her Ilesh and wrote a song in her honor.

Mary was not the only entity that resided in the buildings that now make up O'Flaherty's Irish Channel Pub. Joseph Bapentier and Angelique were there as well. Both were very active with Ghost Expedition participants.

Angelique was consistently the most active with Ghost Expedition participants. It was commonplace for her to walk amongst the participants and for those who couldn't see her, they were able to measure and record a large mobile, yet contained, cold spot. It was easy to detect her cold against the often hot and muggy weather conditions of New Orleans. She was often drawn to young men and children, stroking their hair and holding their hands. Angelique always appeared to look about 20 years old, with waist long, straight brown hair.

Angelique's death produced a bizarre phenomenon. Above the brick planter in the courtyard, formerly the well in which her body was thrown, about two inches above the dirt, there was a moving cold spot the size of an adult hand. The cold was similar to that of the cold associated with the presence of entities, a dry ice feel to it. This was determined to be residual energy from Angelique, although her body was washed away long ago. Even the most skeptical of Ghost Expedition participants could feel the moving circle of cold, especially when the weather was warm.

O'Flaherty's courtyard. The carriageway is located to the left.

Bapentier's presence was often noted too, but not welcomed. He created emotional upset and anger among the visitors in the courtyard. To study the property further regarding the emotional upheaval that Bapentier caused, ISPR Investigators would pose as tourists and sit in the almost-empty courtyard. The scenario was similar case after case: tourists would walk into the courtyard and within moments, begin fighting for no apparent reason. Once out of the property, those questioned had no explanation for the upset in the courtyard. Bapentier, who always manifested an image of a tall, fat man with very little hair and overall oily facial features, was also often physical with visitors by pushing and scratching. Residual images of Bapentier's suicide by hanging were observed on any given day or night.

In October of 1995, Dr. Montz conducted a training course for new Ghost Expedition Researchers. Two investigators accompanied the group. In the courtyard, Angelique implored telepathically to one of the investigators, Maria, to stay outside, not to enter the building. Her presence set off the magnetometer and the cold generated was recorded as a seventeen-degree drop in temperature around Maria. Clairvoyantly, it was obvious that Bapentier was on site, in the building.

Dr. Montz led the group into the empty Ballad Room. Through an entrance to a staircase used only by employees, the group made its way to the vacant second-floor balcony. Outside the heavy wooden doors, Maria began to shiver. "He's mad at me for speaking to Angelique." The group hesitated for a moment, and proceeded through the doors into the balcony area above the Ballad Room. When the group stopped walking, Maria was standing between Dr. Montz and the other investigator while the researchers were standing behind. Suddenly and without warning, a gust of wind blew through the entire group and Maria gasped as Bapentier physically assaulted her and knocked her onto her back on the floor. She was out cold. Dr. Montz bent over the investigator as the others circled around her body on the floor. Dr. Montz lifted Maria's head and shoulders, and within a minute, she came to. Back on her feet again, Maria complained that her throat hurt. She pulled on the collar of her shirt and the group witnessed very dark marks around her neck resembling that of rope burns. Her neck was physically hot to the touch and the bruising lasted twenty-four hours.

On December 17, 1995, one of the ISPR investigators conducted that evening's Ghost Expedition. At O'Flaherty's, the participants were scattered throughout the courtyard. One woman ran over to the investigator, begging her to run back over to the patio section. There, the investigator found another woman, sitting next to her husband, bordering on a state of shock. The woman held her arm out to the investigator and pulled her sleeve back. There, on her forearm, were depressions from an unseen hand squeezing the woman's skin. Her skin was pushed up between each unseen finger and the skin beneath was colorless while the surrounding skin was dark red. Heat was emanating from the woman's arm, and she began to become more emotionally upset. The investigator pulled her into a standing position, and with the assistance of her husband, ushered the woman back out onto Toulouse Street.

Half of the participants followed suit, while the others remained, hoping they too could feel Bapentier's grip. After settling the woman down, the investigator went back to the courtyard to collect the rest of the group and insisted that they leave, against their protests. The investigator explained that in circumstances such as these, they were dealing with the entity of a murderer. This was not the place to push paranormal activity to the limits. After joining the first half of the group on Toulouse Street, the woman who felt Bapentier's vice-like hold begged to leave. It was not unusual to loose a participant or two on Ghost Expeditions through O'Flaherty's.

During an afternoon Ghost Expedition at O'Flaherty's in February 1996, one male participant, about forty years of age, became enraged in the courtyard. He yelled at the researcher, accusing her of telling lies about ghosts and hauntings of O'Flaherty's and that she didn't know what she was speaking about. The Ghost Expedition participants were stunned. They stood perfectly still as the man continued to scream at the researcher, and as he began walking towards her as if to attack, several of the participants blocked him with their bodies. Two men in the group walked the angry man back out onto Toulouse Street. The researcher waited a minute and then led the rest out as well. On the street, the man looked completely shocked, and apologized profusely to the researcher. He had no idea why his attitude and demeanor changed so drastically, something he claimed was not indicative of his true personality. But the researcher knew why. Bapentier had struck again.

The security bars on the third-floor windows were installed during the 1800s. During the epidemics that swept through the French Quarter, when the third floor was used as a quarantine area for victims, those who were ill tried repeatedly to jump from the windows to the courtyard three floors below to bring an end to their suffering. Instead, bars were installed to prevent these victims from leaping to their deaths. Today, the third floor has very heavy residual energy from the hundreds of those who died within those walls.

In May of 1996, Danny O'Flaherty complained that the haunted status of his property was prompting complaints from many of his parish priests. To assist, the clairvoyant investigators from the ISPR remotely cleared the property of its entities. Several on-site visits were made by the ISPR investigators to O'Flaherty's, and during each visit, neither scientific nor clairvoyant findings indicated that the property was still actively haunted. Even the cold spot documented for years at the site of the former well was gone. O'Flaherty's was taken off the ISPR Ghost Expedition Property list.

Shortly after the clearing and subsequent investigator visits, the new publicity manager of O'Flaherty's contacted the ISPR and requested that O'Flaherty's be placed back on the Ghost Expedition property list, for business was down. ISPR could not honor this request as the property showed no indication of paranormal activity. Many months later, Dr. Montz line produced a New Orleans segment for the Rysher television series, *Strange Universe,* featuring several ISPR-investigated sites in the French Quarter. The publicity manager for O'Flaherty's was the local producer. Without obtaining permission from Dr. Montz or Rysher, she slipped in a quick interview with Danny O'Flaherty, having him claim that the pub was again haunted—that *the ghosts came back because they like his music!* Just goes to prove you can't believe *everything* you see on television about the paranormal. The ISPR was not asked to investigate the property again, and today, a fictional New Orleans ghost/vampire tour originates from the courtyard of O'Flaherty's.

Rendering of Angelique during a 1995 Ghost Expedition.

Rendering of Joseph Bapentier during a 1995 Ghost Expedition.

Omni Royal Orleans Hotel
621 St. Louis Street

The storytellers and buggy drivers of New Orleans love to add to the real history of the city to make a more exciting story. One of their favorite fabrications revolves around Maspero's Restaurant. They claim it is the original site of Maspero's Slave Exchange, though it wasn't. The Omni Royal Orleans Hotel, located across the street, was. Currently, the hotel is haunted by the ghost of a former maid. Paranormal phenomena is most prevalent on the second floor. Air conditioning, heat, and water faucets turn on and off by themselves, and phones ring with no one on the other line. ISPR investigations of many New Orleans Hotels have revealed the same kinds of phenomena.

In July of 1995, I stayed in room 227 of the Omni Royal Orleans Hotel for one week, while working on several New Orleans investigations with the ISPR Team. Each night, I answered my ringing phone repeatedly, only to be met with a steady hiss on the line. The front desk assured me that no outside call came through the switchboard, nor were these phone calls internal, one hotel room to another.

On the second day of my stay, the hotel housekeeper made up my room before I left. When she was through, we both exited and I left the hotel to attend a breakfast for the ISPR investigators. Afterward, we had several hours of free time available. The outside temperature in the French Quarter rose above one hundred degrees before 11 a.m. I decided to spend my free hours at the rooftop pool. I had to stop back at my room and change into the appropriate attire, and as I placed my card key into my hotel room door, I heard water running inside. I opened the door, entered my bathroom and saw that the faucet was running at full blast. I could have sworn that when the hotel maid and I had left my room, everything was shut off. Without thinking, I reached for the cold water faucet and turned the water off. At that point, I figured that it must have been water pressure that had turned the faucet on in the first place.

Later that afternoon, I returned to my hotel room. The water was running as I opened the door. Again, the cold water faucet was on full blast. I turned it off and forgot about it.

On the last day of my visit in New Orleans, I walked into my bathroom for the last time. As I closed the door behind me, the cold water faucet turned on *as I watched*. Stunned for a moment, I watched the water fall. I leaned over and turned the faucet off. Within three seconds, the faucet turned back on. Again, I turned the water off. And again, I watched it turn on; this time with such a force that it made the water spew out. Without further prompting, I shouted at the sink, "I just want to use the bathroom with some privacy, can you give me a minute?" To my utter shock and amazement, the cold water faucet turned all the way off and remained that way until I left the room.

When I relocated to New Orleans to join the ISPR Team in its six-year study of hauntings in the city, I made acquaintances with many of the desk staff and concierge at the Omni. Room 227, according to the hotel staff, continues to have problems and usually doesn't keep the same guests for more than one night.

Royal Cafe

700 Royal Street

The Royal Cafe, also known as the LaBranche House, is heralded as the most photographed building in New Orleans. The four-story structure was built in 1832 by Jean Baptiste LaBranche, a wealthy sugar planter. LaBranche was formerly known as Zweig in his native Germany. When Zweig came to New Orleans and tried to register with Immigration, the French immigration officer could not understand his name. In frustration, Zweig dragged the officer outside, broke off a tree branch and waved it at the officer as he repeated, "Zweig! Zweig!" The confused officer looked at Zweig and said, "ah, Monsieur LaBranche!" Years later, Zweig bought a plantation upriver and named it the LaBranche Planation. LaBranche learned that a rose by any other name *would* smell as sweet!

It was well known that LaBranche enjoyed himself in mixed company that did not include his wife. As long as LaBranche was alive, his wife put up with his continuous infidelities. After LaBranche died in 1842, his wife sought out her husband's most recent mistress, Melissa. Mrs. LaBranche tricked the young woman into following her up to the fourth floor, where the widow knocked her out with a blow to the head and chained her up to the wall. There, the young Melissa died a slow death from starvation.

The Royal Cafe and several apartments in the adjoining buildings were all investigated by the ISPR Team. During each investigation, Investigators found evidence of Mrs. LaBranche. Further post-investigative research revealed that LaBranche had also owned the adjoining buildings. Mrs. LaBranche does not disturb anything in these apartments, but she is often seen walking from room to room.

In the Royal Cafe however, Mrs. LaBranche's presence is strong, especially on the second floor. Many dining guests of the restaurant report an overwhelming sensation that someone, a female, is standing right behind them, watching them intently.

And the mistress, Melissa? She's at the Royal Cafe too. Her presence is more often noticed in the administrative offices. A former female Royal Cafe manager was befriended by Melissa, who appeared to entertain herself by borrowing extra shoes and other personal items out of the manager's office. The manager soon learned not to blame the other employees for her missing items. One day, after reprimanding the entire kitchen and waitstaff for violating her privacy and taking her personal items, she retreated back to her office upstairs. At her desk, she was still angry and muttered aloud, "how do I catch them at it?" Her question was quickly replied by a coffee mug that sat on one end of her desk being tossed across the desk right in front of her. The manager realized that the thefts must have been Melissa's doing, so she asked out loud. Her answer came in the form of gentle fingers brushing her bangs off her forehead. From that day forward, Melissa had permission to go through the manager's items in her office, and ever since, when items were missing during the day, they were returned by nightfall.

The LaBranche Building is one of the most photographed in the French Quarter.

San Francisco Plantation

Reserve, Louisiana

The San Francisco Plantation in Reserve, Louisiana, was built in 1856 by Edmond Bozonier Marmillion. The plantation was originally named Sans Fruscins, meaning, "without a penny in my pocket." Marmillion and his wife had three sons, Pierre, Antoine, and Charles. In 1870, Antoine and Charles bought all the interests in the plantation. Antoine and his wife, Louise, had three daughters and Charles never married. In 1871, Antoine died, leaving his wife and Charles to run the plantation. Charles, after suffering poor health for years, passed away in 1875. Louise sold the plantation in 1879 to Achille D. Bourgere and moved her family to Germany. Bourgere renamed the plantation San Francisco. The two-story Creole-style house boasts of advanced mid-nineteenth century design, which was restored in the mid-1970s for a cool $2,000,000.

Is it haunted? Jennifer, the plantation Operations Manager, wanted to know for sure. She contacted the ISPR. As standard operating procedure, parapsychologist Dr. Larry Montz requested that she not divulge any information about the haunting activities. The investigation took place on a warm afternoon at 4:00 pm.

The last tour group was being led through the plantation home as the parapsychologist and investigators were ushered upstairs to wait. Antique treasures were on display throughout the living quarters on the second floor. Jennifer met the team on the second floor and led them to the attic where a large ballroom had been planned but was never completed. Panels along the perimeter were originally designed to open up to allow fresh air to circulate. Photos were shot, environmental and electro-magnetic readings were taken, however, no paranormal activity was noted. The clairvoyant investigators noted that the only residual impressions received were those of children who used to reside in the house and play in the attic.

On the second floor, however, the clairvoyant investigators picked up on several impressions of a gentleman dying in one of the bedrooms to the left of the house, over the kitchen area. They described the man to be in his mid-thirties, a cigar smoker with severe chest problems; his name was *Charles*. As the clairvoyant information was spoken out loud, the temperature of the bedroom dropped significantly. Two of the investigators immediately stated that they felt the presence of an entity in the house and suggested that it was a male. The team proceeded through the other second-floor rooms and described residuals of children playing, as well as one little girl suffering an ill-

ness in another bedroom. High electro-magnetic readings were taken in the second-floor parlor and seemed to be associated with the energy from the male entity.

Throughout the ground floor, the clairvoyant investigators received impressions of numerous slaves at work. Dr. Montz recorded a high electro-magnetic field in the dining room, also seemingly associated with the male entity. To the far right of the house, on the main floor, was a room with brick walls and iron bars on the windows. The team instantly felt that it was originally used as an office of some sort, a place were money was counted. Dr.

Is it a ghost? No. Dr. Montz caught an investigator on film instead.

Montz recorded electro-magnetic readings that were incredibly high without any rational explanation, and the temperature dropped dramatically. Two clairvoyant investigators announced that a male entity was indeed present, standing in the corner and again offered the name of Charles. Again, they described him but with greater detail. He had reddish-brown hair, a mustache, was of medium build and wearing a long brown coat. Immediately, Jennifer spoke up and admitted that he was the same man she has seen at the plantation and agreed that it was Charles, one of the three sons of the original builder of the San Francisco Planation.

At the end of the ISPR investigation, the team concluded that there was one conscious entity present at the San Francisco Plantation, the ghost of Charles Marmillion. Post-investigative research through historical records further substantiated his existence at the plantation. It was discovered that Charles was indeed a cigar smoker who died after suffering for many years with chest problems. The team's assessment of the main-floor room with bars on the windows proved to be Charles' office, were he did count money. He could be remaining in the house due to his untimely death at the age of 35.

The San Francisco Plantation is located less that an hour's drive west of New Orleans. Daily tours are offered between 10:00 am and 4:00 pm.

The view from the attic balcony afforded an incredible view of the plantation's grounds.

ISPR found the entity of Charles Marmillion still present at the San Francisco Plantation. *Courtesy of San Francisco Plantation.*

Shalimar Indian Cuisine
535 Wilkinson Row

Shalimar Indian Cuisine takes up two floors of the building on Wilkinson Row, which was constructed in 1895 and originally a Jax Brewery warehouse. The building was not known to be active with paranormal phenomena until the current owners took over the property in order to open a restaurant. The entity that has been found inside the building has no connection with the property itself. Instead, this entity is an Indian Zeik, a holy man who protects the family. He is often seen wearing a turban and long robes and carries a large curved sword. On the second floor, people sometimes feel a large presence standing behind them, accompanied by a drastic drop in temperature. Former waiters report that when they arrived in the morning to set up the lunch buffet, it was common to find the chairs moved away from the tables and the silverware in disarray upon the tabletops. Frequently during lunch, which is served on the second floor, customers hear what sounds like heavy furniture being dragged across the floor above them. The third floor, however, is only used for storage.

Shalimar Indian Cuisine was a frequent nighttime Ghost Expedition location. Ghost Expeditions could enter the building and go directly to the second floor, as dinners are served on the first floor. On March 24, 1997, a Ghost Expedition researcher took her group into Shalimar and directly upstairs to the second floor. In the middle of explaining just what a *Zeik* is, a large dark shadow superimposed the researcher while the group stood witness. The researcher reacted in a threatened manner and backed up across the entire dining room and came to a stop up against the far wall, as the shadow remained in contact. Three participants ran from the dining room and down the stairs back out to the street. The rest of the group stood in frozen in a state of fear and shock. The researcher, finally finding her voice, apologized out loud for possibly verbalizing anything that was not accurate. The apology seemed to do the trick, as the shadow moved back off the researcher and dissipated.

In August of 1996, a gentleman from Salt Lake City participated in a evening Ghost Expedition. He took photographs of each property, including Shalimar. He took three photographs of the old Jax Brewery Warehouse building. When he had his photographs developed, he discovered that his camera had captured anomalies. The gentleman sent his photographs and the negatives to the ISPR for analysis. The ISPR concluded that indeed, anomalies were captured on film in front of Shalimar Indian Cuisine.

Shalimar Indian Cuisine restaurant

Just because the dining room was closed didn't mean that it was empty.

When first constructed, the building was a former Jax Brewery warehouse.

Police sketch artist Renee Spar's perception and drawing of the Zeik matched those provided by ISPR investigations as well as Ghost Expedition participants.

Rick Lee, from Utah, captures the beginning of paranormal phenomena on film, during an August 1996 Ghost Expedition in front of Shalimar Indian Cuisine.

The second photo in the series, shows the paranormal phenomena is still taking place.

The third photo in the series shows nothing out of the ordinary.

The three-photo series became an identifying logo for ISPR's New Orleans Ghost Expeditions.

St. Pierre Hotel
Burgundy Street

The St. Pierre Hotel's lodging buildings are situated on both sides of Burgundy Street, formally known as Craps. The complex is actually comprised of houses, slave quarters, and buildings moved from other locations around the French Quarter. The hotel lobby is located inside an original house which has been standing on this street for over a hundred years. A sizable portion of the hotel incorporates eleven slave quarters originally from Iberville and Bienville Streets. These eleven buildings were relocated to their present site on the northeast corner of the French Quarter due to D.H. Holmes, Ltd. The corporation slowly purchased the city blocks during the time frame of 1916 into the 1950s in order to build the department store of the same name.

The owner of the St. Pierre Hotel contacted the ISPR because of reports of unexplained events taking place in different rooms. The investigation was conducted at 11:00 p.m. one night in mid-September 1996. It took several hours to enter each building in order to take atmospheric readings as well as allow the clairvoyant investigators to get their impressions.

The team found the residual impressions fascinating because of the vast mixture of energy from the site itself and the relocated buildings. Electronically, the team found several areas with high electro-magnetic energy fields as well as cold spots of dramatic temperature variations.

In each building, the clairvoyant investigators received residual impressions of individuals who have lived in the houses and buildings that are original to this location. Interestingly enough, the team found that the transplanted slave quarter buildings were clear of any paranormal phenomena or residual impressions.

The team did find two active entities on site at the St. Pierre Hotel. The appearance of the first entity provided a simultaneous scientific and psychic hit. As the meters began to register activity, two of the investigators saw a black man standing in the carriageway next to the main lobby. He appeared to be between forty-five and fifty years of age, medium build, wearing a royal blue-colored shirt and pants. He was merely standing still, looking out to the street. As the team moved closer with the equipment, the cameras failed to fire. His presence then dissipated.

The second entity discovered was a Civil War Confederate soldier in a slave quarter behind an old school house, across the street from the hotel lobby. This slave quarter structure has one large bedroom and bathroom upstairs. There have been reports of a black shadow, unusual coldness and an apparition of a man in gray, usually viewed at the foot of the bed. The ISPR Team was able to record the story of a paranormal event in this room directly from an eyewitness. The following is her recollection from our taped interview with her.

"I have been staying here for two nights to attend a convention, I'm from San Francisco. The first night, I went to dinner, came back to the room and noticed that my clothes were out of my suitcase on the bed. I thought it was a little strange because I didn't remember taking them out, but I just blew it off and didn't think about it anymore. The only other thing that I thought was strange was the fact that my TV set would change channels from wherever I placed it...it would return to channel 7. I turned off the TV and went to sleep. But last night was the topper. After dinner, I returned to my room and turned on the TV. It was really late and I started getting ready for bed. I was in the bathroom washing up and I heard the TV changing channels. It frightened me, so I peeked out of the bathroom. I didn't see anyone but I felt like someone was watching me. I finished up in the bathroom and turned off the TV and got into bed. Just as I started to go to sleep, I actually felt something sit on my bed and move next to me. I could feel the bed depress like someone really sat down. I didn't know what to do and in a moment, I started to get ice cold even though I was lying under the covers. I got goose bumps and couldn't move until I felt the touch of a hand or something on my leg...it was ice cold! I jumped out of bed and ran into the courtyard!"

It is the opinion of the ISPR Team that it was the Confederate Soldier who tried to entertain this St. Pierre Hotel guest. During the interview, Dr. Montz asked the witness if this was a negative experience for her. She said that actually, it was kind of thrilling. She was taken by surprise and that's why she fled from her room, but it was the highlight of her trip to New Orleans and gave her something to talk about for a long time to come.

── Southern Nights Bed & Breakfast ──
Uptown District

In the Spring of 1996, I received a call from Judy Garwood, the owner of Southern Nights Bed & Breakfast, located on Carrolton in the Uptown District of New Orleans. Judy knew about the ISPR Ghost Expeditions, and was putting together a new weekend package for her guests and wanted to include something that was real regarding the paranormal. She invited me over to meet and to see her house, which she had just completed renovating.

When I arrived, Judy met me at the left front door. What should have been a huge living room was Judy's office. After speaking about business, Judy invited me to join her for some coffee and dessert in the dining room; which is

After participating in a Ghost Expedition in the French Quarter, actress Delta Burke was ready to investigate ghosts all night long during the Premiere ISPR Overnight Ghost Expedition at the Southern Nights mansion.

The Southern Nights Mansion sits on the historic New Orleans Streetcar line.

located in the bed & breakfast part of the house. We sat at a large dining room table which was already set with fancy china and flatware, ready to accomodate a party of ten. Shortly into my second cup of coffee, Judy was speaking and my attention was drawn to the doorway opening up into the service hallway between the kitchen and dining room. I saw what I thought was a woman drift out of the doorway and through the dining room over to the wall butler, and then simply disappear. Judy asked me if I noticed that it got colder in the dining room, which brought my attention back. It did feel colder. I asked Judy if she ever experienced any paranormal activity in this house. She looked kind of surprised at the question, but was excited that I asked. She went on to tell me about all the times her alarm systems would go off in the house, even though no one else was there. She and her son would hear their names being called out when they were home, alone. Locked doors would open. Open doors would close and lock. She had a great wealth of experiences to share.

That's what prompted Judy Garwood to retain the ISPR for a paranormal investigation of the Southern Nights Bed & Breakfast.

The Southern Nights Bed & Breakfast is a mansion of over 7,000 square feet, on three floors. The guest side of the mansion is over 3,700 square feet. The property, now completely renovated, dates back to the 1800s and is located on New Orleans' historic street car line. There are gorgeous hardwood floors throughout with stylishly high ceilings, crown molding and thirteen coal burning fireplaces.

Downstairs in the owner's side of the haunted mansion, there are separate owner's quarters, including a forty-foot long front parlor, a library with custom-built, floor-to-ceiling book units, family Room, bedroom with private full bath, separate entrances from outside and inside to the magazine picture-perfect kitchen and elegant dining room and adjoining bed-and-breakfast living room. The guest side of the mansion has ten bedrooms as well as a newly remodeled, 70-foot-long third-floor apartment, complete with a full kitchen, full bath, hardwood floors, ten-foot-high ceilings, polished hardwood floors, and three beautiful skylights.

The private and secured back yard of the mansion has three separate decks. Access to the landscaped decks are from the owner's side, bed-and-breakfast side, and the third-floor apartment.

During the first ISPR Team investigation of the mansion, the team identified three entities. The first was an adult female named Cecilia. Information garnered clairvoyantly during this investigation suggested that she was the wife of the builder of the mansion. The other was a young girl, apparently Cecilia's daughter. The third was a man in a green leisure suit, who did not appear to have an obvious connection with the property. Cecilia and the little girl are the most active in the mansion. Hardly has there been a guest who stayed at the Southern Nights Bed & Breakfast without encountering one or both of these entities. Most guests tell Judy at breakfast how their bedroom doors wouldn't stay closed and locked and items were moved while they weren' t looking.

The ISPR featured Southern Nights on *National Geographic Explorer* and a special on the Discovery Channel, *America's Haunted Houses*. During the filming of *America's Haunted Houses*, Dr. Montz took the film crew upstairs into Bedroom Two. While Dr. Montz was speaking about paranormal field research, the temperature of the room dropped significantly. As the film crew began to notice the temperature drop, Dr. Montz pointed to the bed. In front of the entire film crew, a depression was made on the bed as if an adult sat down. And indeed, an adult did, it was Cecilia. Bedroom 2 is one of her favorites; Dr. Montz knew that ahead of time.

Southern Nights proved to be an incredible property for paranormal research. In addition to the ISPR television specials shot at Southern Nights, the ISPR began using the mansion for its brand new Overnight Ghost Expeditions. Many people participated in the two years they were conducted, the Premiere Overnight Ghost Expedition even had actress Delta Burke participate. It was only fitting for the last Overnight Ghost Expedition to have a celebrity, and it did—Robbi Chong of *Poltergeist: The Legacy*. The following article, written by Jillian, a clairvoyant, was published in the *Hauntings Today* newsletter.

ISPR investigator Daena Smoller originally saw Cecelia,
a female entity, in the mansion's dining room.

Ghosts & Celebrities: The Premiere ISPR Overnight Ghost Expedition

On September 27, 1996, the ISPR made it possible for those interested in paranormal research to experience the ultimate haunting. It was the debut of the ISPR Overnight Ghost Expedition, an all-night, mini-investigation of a haunted mansion in New Orleans with an experienced ISPR investigator and necessary equipment. For the first Overnight Ghost Expedition, parapsychologist Dr. Larry Montz and four ISPR Investigators were in attendance along with ten people of varying backgrounds. Dr. Montz and student investigator, Ed, arrived prior to the investigation participants to install additional motion detectors on the second floor which contains ten rooms. Investigator Daena Smoller and I installed special low lights on the 70-foot-long third floor. There was already activity taking place, a shadow beneath the third floor bathroom door (the bathroom light was not on). One of the entities manifested itself in front of us moments later, and the doors on the second floor that had been left open shut and locked without any visible assistance.

The Overnight Ghost Expedition participants began arriving at 10:30 pm. We even had a celebrity, actress Delta Burke. All the participants wanted to be Delta's research partner that night, so Dr. Montz wisely chose a woman who flew in from California who worked in the entertainment industry. Once everyone arrived, we enjoyed a delicious buffet, although most of the participants were too excited and anxious to taste their food. Afterward, equipment and research paperwork was assigned to each team of two. Next, each team drew a room key out of a box for their first assigned location. The plan called for each team to spend forty minutes in each room with a twenty-minute break in between. Briefed on investigation techniques that were to be applied for the evening, the teams were ushered to their designated locations and once inside, motion detectors in the hallways were set.

The forty minutes passed quickly for ISPR investigators who remained on the main floor. We couldn't wait to see their faces during the first break. We weren't disappointed—Delta and Molly reported a drastic drop in temperature in Room Two, coupled with a distinct feeling of being watched. Heather and Pamela, in Room One, noted that they initially could not resist the urge to giggle and that the left corner of the door to another room was lit for the first half of the session, and then it turned off. They recorded on their Data Collection Forms that they heard a female shriek and a dull pounding on the floor. George and Marti, while in Room Three, also documented "we heard what sounded like a loud cry or scream in the hallway".

There is another living room of equal size on the other side of the staircase wall. The mansion has over 7,500 square feet and a tri-level deck in the private backyard.

Don and Tony, who were stationed by themselves on the third floor, were unusually quiet. Later, both men revealed the fact that they had seen an apparition of a man in a suit. Their description matched the entity found during the first ISPR investigation, some months back. There was a great deal of talking and giggling and the twenty minute break flew by. Time already to usher the participants to their new locations. Secured in their new posts, the motion detectors in the hallways were switched back on.

Break two reports were also remarkable. Heather and Pamela were in the room previously occupied by Delta and Molly and reported extremely cold temperatures. Delta and Molly, in a new room, described a bright white light emanating from under the door that connected to another room. Later in the night, Marti and George recorded that they too saw a white light beneath the door in the same room, as well as flashes of light in the hallway and on the wall. They stated that the light in the other room had been off the entire time.

Marti and George were on the third floor for this shift. Marti reported a white cloud and upon moving closer, saw the outline of a little girl. A roving red dot on the screen saver of a computer made them take notice. They witnessed a large orange dot that appeared to roam all over the middle of the screen. At times, it would change to a blue color. Upon close inspection, the computer turned out to be a TV set, which was unplugged to boot!

In the 3:00 a.m. hour, three teams reported hearing footsteps in the hallway, outside of their rooms, yet the motion detectors were not triggered.

The break during the 4:00 a.m. hour was active with paranormal phenomenon for everyone as a group. As Dr. Montz was revealing what we know about the entities that reside in the mansion, a small cold spot was noted by an investigation participant, standing in the middle of the floor. Participants crowded around to feel the icy cold and tingling sensations, and watch the meters dance. The cold spot moved twice and all were able to follow its path around the room.

Once more, the investigation participants ascended the stairs for their new locations. This time, there were more reports of moving cold spots, tingling sensations, and audible footsteps in the hallways. Marti reported that she got a quick image of a tailor's dress form sporting a velvet dress with an empire waist. This was amazing since this tailor's dress form actually exists in the owner's private quarters, rooms to which no one had access. Delta and Molly found their room locked upon trying to leave for the next break and had to be rescued.

Throughout the entire night, strange phenomena occurred, amazing and exhilerating to our Overnight Ghost Expedition participants. At 7:30 a.m., an alarm clock bell began to scream in the seventh bedroom, which was unoccupied. Upon examination, we found it unplugged without a back-up battery. I simply pushed the off switch and the alarm immediately ceased. A fitting end to the incredibly active Premiere ISPR Overnight Ghost Expedition.

The following article was published in the November/December 1997 issue of the *ISPR Journal*.

Grand Finale: New Orleans Overnight Ghost Expedition with MGM's *Poltergeist: The Legacy* Winners and Actress Robbi Chong, by Daena Smoller

The plans were put into motion in February of 1997. In an effort to promote the MGM television series, *Poltergeist: The Legacy*, a national Enter-to-Win sweepstakes would take place during September and October and the grand prize winners would participate in an Overnight Ghost Expedition at the ISPR Haunted Mansion in New Orleans over Halloween weekend. Last February, no one thought that it would be the last Overnight Ghost Expedition that the ISPR would conduct in that city. As the ISPR Investigative Team relocated to Los Angeles during the summer of 1997, and as the violence in the city of New Orleans escalated, discussion of making the MGM Overnight Ghost Expedition the last to be conducted became more prevalent. By the end of the summer, ISPR evaluated the research data collected in New Orleans over the last three years and the decision was made: close the New Orleans operation completely and make the MGM Overnight Ghost Expedition a Grand Finale Celebration.

The six Grand Prize Winners and their guests were flown to New Orleans

Footsteps are heard at random times by the mansion's
owner, Judy Garwood, and her son Ben

courtesy of MGM Domestic Television. Upon arriving, the ISPR set the winners up for the first night at the Bourbon Orleans Hotel in the French Quarter of New Orleans. On Saturday, the winners participated in a New Orleans Ghost Expedition Level I and were awarded with passes to take a Millennium French Quarter Walking Tour and passes to the Aquarium of the Americas.

At 10:30 pm, the winners congregated at the New Orleans Ghost Expedition Office. Student Investigator Ed was preparing to work his final Expedition. Ed rounded up the winners and by streetcar, the group traveled to the historic haunted mansion that had been utilized for Overnight Ghost Expeditions for little more than a year. Upon arrival at the mansion, Ed kept his group outside the brick wall and conducted a small remote viewing exercise. Armed with notebooks and pens, the group tried to project their energy into the mansion to remotely see the interior. They wrote down their descriptions, and it was discovered later that at least half the group accurately described details of the mansion's interior. It must be noted that from the outside, one can see how deep the mansion stands on the property. So descriptions of long hallways and a lot of wood (it *is* New Orleans) can also be interpreted as educated guesses and not necessarily successful remote viewing. But the winners enjoyed the experiment!

Once inside, I introduced myself to the entire group and laid out the itinerary for the night's paranormal investigation of the mansion. Being somewhat of a ham (I was a radio on-air personality for sixteen years), I found myself having a good time entertaining—hey, it's kind of like having your own paranormal party! In addition to the winners, Kendra Bradley from MGM Domestic Television and Robbie Chong from *Poltergeist: The Legacy*, were also in attendance. I took the entire group on an informal tour of the mansion first. I wanted them to get familiar with exactly where they were; it helps participants to decipher paranormal activity from real activity during the investigation. I took them through all three floors, through every one of the ten bedrooms, seven and a half baths, living rooms, dining room and kitchen. I pointed out all thirteen fireplaces and all the other interesting points of the mansion. Back downstairs in the dining room, we broke out the feast that the owner prepared. Judy did a beautiful job of putting together two hundred finger sandwiches, homemade red beans and rice, cookies, and beverages. The group ate very quickly; they were eager to begin.

We moved into one of the living rooms and I conducted a very unorthodox ESP test. Instead of the one-on-one test that is conducted for research, I had everyone concentrate on the Zenner Testing card being held up, then had everyone write down their answers. To take myself off the spot, I volunteered Kendra to hold each card and concentrate on putting that information out to the group in a telepathic manner (hey, if the group didn't do well, they couldn't blame me!). As a result, the group of winners didn't do too badly, not great, but not too badly. Ed however, didn't get one right! Robbie Chong never volunteered her results. It was hysterical.

ISPR investigator Daena Smoller is thrilled to pose with actress Robbi Chong before the Grand Finale ISPR Overnight Ghost Expedition at the Southern Nights mansion, sponsored by MGM's *Poltergeist: The Legacy* television series.

It was now time to distribute the equipment and explain why each piece is used. I made the mistake of teasing the group with a couple of details of a Los Angeles investigation that ISPR now refers to only as *Hell House*. Robbie Chong wanted to know about the investigation NOW! The group of winners supported her demand. I had no problem with this; I always get a kick out of seeing the looks on all the faces each time I speak about this investigation. Ed rolled his eyes to the ceiling. He wasn't in Los Angeles for this investigation. After all the *Oh my Gods* and *Ewwweees*, it was time to begin the last paranormal investigation of the ISPR New Orleans Haunted Mansion. The group was broken down into two paranormal teams, each receiving the same equipment. Ed took his group to the second floor to start, I marched my group right up to the third floor, suspecting that it was going to be fairly active and neither my group nor I were disappointed.

As we neared the end of the second floor hallway at the door of the last bedroom, one of my team members, a pretty blonde girl from Missouri, looked like she was going to cry. She did the same earlier, during the tour of the mansion, in the same place. I looked at her and she assured me that she was okay. We exited the second-floor door at the back of the mansion, walked out through the landing, and through another door to a stairwell. The stairwell led us upstairs to the third floor. I opened the door gently, as to not disturb the energy. My group filtered in behind me into the newly designed third-floor kitchen, with equipment in hand. The third floor, however, is seventy feet long and with minimal lighting. It appears to disappear into nothingness at the other end.

Huddled together in the kitchenette, my team members began taking temperature readings and electro-magnetic readings. The temperature gauges proved that it was slightly chilly, around 72 degrees. No significant electro-magnetic readings were detected. And as a backup, the compasses read exactly the way they should. For fun, but not a scientific tool, we brought along a set dousing rods. The rods remained still. No real psychic impressions were noted at this point, yet I could definitely feel the quiet, anticipatory energy from my team. I already liked my group a great deal!

We moved past the kitchenette, through a more narrow hallway. The full bath takes up three-quarters of the space, helping to break up the room. On the other side of bathroom and hallway there was a full-sized bed with bedroom furniture on either side. Past that, there was a living room area and then an exercise room. It was, however, all open and separated by the furniture arrangements. Between the bathroom and the bed, we all came to a dead stop. The area around us seemed to drop in temperature and the girl who looked like she was going to cry before started making faces. We were all waving our hands around, amazed by the cold, until I reminded them that we have equipment—we should use it! A temperature gauge was thrust into what appeared to be the middle of the cold, and sure enough, our physical sense to the cold was correct. Out came the magnetometer and squeals of delight accompanied the oscillating meter needle. It was exciting to watch the compass needle spin out of control, like it was more than just a little confused. One team member remembered that he held the dousing rods and stood back from the group to extend his arms while holding the rods. The right rod spun quickly to face him directly. A little shocked, he brought the group's attention to this and the remaining equipment was quickly directed at him. The temperature dropped further, the compass still behaved as a crazy person trapped in an all-white room with no doors, and the oscillating needle on the magnetometer continued its bizarre movement higher on the scale. At that point, the Missouri girl began to cry.

We moved a couple of feet over to the bed and the crying Missouri girl sat down. I sat down facing her, trying to reassure her that she was experiencing some kind of empathic episode and hopefully we would be able to garner more information as the night continued. Another woman began to cry, and yet another. It might have appeared to be contagious, as is laughter amongst strangers. This was my original thought until they volunteered a girl's name at the same time. The three felt a tightening in their chests and a closed-in feeling. I was feeling it too, but never volunteered the information; I was delighted. As the women spoke the name over and over, they each, in turn, felt someone unseen hold their hand, the temperature dropped three more degrees and the poles pointed steadily at the three women. The magnetometer and compass continued to do their dances.

The Missouri girl could not stop crying. I was torn between moving her so she would stop crying, and leaving her in hopes of more information. The part of my mind which controls my own thoughts of vanity chimed in.

Overnight Ghost Expedition winners from across the United States are excited to participate in a Ghost Expedition with a Hollywood celebrity.

Since everyone's eyes would be swollen and red from staying up all night, why move? So we didn't and we were rewarded with more information over the next forty-five minutes. Each of the women felt that there was a presence of a young girl (the entity of this young girl has shown up during each and every Overnight Ghost Expedition in the haunted mansion), who was punished for something and made to stay by herself in a room as punishment. What crime exactly the young girl had committed was never revealed.

After a good deal of time on the third floor, my group decided to continue the investigation on the second floor. The last two rooms on the second floor, toward the back of the mansion, also contained very heavy energy, and two of the women refused to enter for they felt a flood of tears threatening to fall again. When my team entered Room Two (which is a favorite for one of the entities; an adult female named Cecilia), we noted immediately that the room was freezing! Three of us sat on edges of the bed, which is in the center of the room, while the rest began to take readings. Without any warning, a side drawer on one of the nightstands popped open as wide as it could, without any visible assistance! Most of us jumped due to the shock value. After regaining our composure, we tested the door on the nightstand. It has an inner, automatic latch that would prevent it from opening without assistance. As we all giggled over the incident and our reactions, the area on the bed between the three of us dropped further in temperature. The magnetometer needle was swinging wildly and several of us began to laugh. Everyone agreed that this was a very pleasant presence. The rest of the investigation of the mansion produced equipment readings and substantiated the psychic impressions of the two entities previously found. The third entity that ISPR had found in the mansion over the last year was not found during this investigation. The entity is of a man and every person who has seen him describes him as wearing a green suit. We don't know what his connection is with the mansion.

In the hour or so before dawn, tired but exhilarated, my team sat downstairs in the living room and discussed all things paranormal until 8:30 am. At that point, the other team joined us in the living room and we all feasted on a delicious brunch. My team was excited to share their findings with the smaller team and to find out what experiences they had. We laughed hysterically when we found out that the other team whisked through a few rooms on the second floor and all passed out on the third around 3:00 a.m.

ISPR would like to thank MGM Domestic Television and *Poltergeist: The Legacy* for teaming up with Ghost Expeditions to make the final New Orleans Overnight Ghost Expedition a tremendous success! And of course, a huge thanks to Judy Garwood who has offered her haunted mansion to be studied by the ISPR Investigative Team.

After the ISPR closed its New Orleans branch on November 1, 1997, Judy Garwood continued to participate in Ghost Expedition promotions. In 1997, 1998 and 1999, Judy's haunted mansion has been the destination stay for the grand prize winners of a Ghost Expedition weekend with an ISPR Investigator in New Orleans, as a wheel prize for the *Wheel of Fortune* and as the second runner-up prize for *Jeopardy!* in 1997. During the first half of June, 1997, Dr. Montz set up an unprecented internet event at Judy's mansion, a *24-Hour Live Chat Room* with the ISPR. Over 8,000 questions were submitted in the first four hours alone. Dr. Montz answered questions for a straight 24 hours, live from the haunted Southern Nights Bed & Breakfast.

The 70-foot attic of the mansion is only accessible by exiting the mansion on the second floor and entering through another door to an enclosed stairwell. It can now function as a full apartment with its kitchen, full bath, beds and living room/library. Skylights allow it to be bright all day.

Two Entities and a Ghost on the Side, Please

Although the term "ghost" is used by the majority of people to describe an entity, in the scientific community, a ghost can refer to a great number of things, including images, sounds as well as sights. An entity, however, is the term the scientific community uses to describe a conscious being, one that was previously alive but no longer has a physical body.

In the interest of pursuing more information about entities, hauntings and the human abilities of Psi in the field, the ISPR conducted almost two hundred investigations during the six-year research study in the city. Many properties, if actively haunted, had just one entity. Such was the case with the Chart House Restaurant, located at 801 Chartres Street at Jackson Square. The building which contains the restaurant is one of the oldest buildings in the French Quarter. Is has seen many changes throughout the years; from schoolhouse to residence to spaghetti factory. ISPR investigations revealed the entity of a man on the second floor. He dresses in late 1800s attire. Most of the time, this entity goes unseen, but that wasn't the case during the early morning hours of one spring day in 1994. A waitress was in the upper floor dining rooms of the Chart House, preparing the tables for the lunch business. While in one intimate room of ten tables, the waitress was bending over the tabletop. She felt a tap on her shoulder and stood up and turned around, expecting to see a kitchen employee. Instead, she saw a man dressed in attire that she did not recognize. In response to her wide eyes, the man simply said, "Hello." Before she could respond, the man faded away from sight. The waitress quit her job before the first patron walked in for lunch.

Ghost Expeditions utilized the Chart House Restaurant, not for its active haunting, but for simple clairvoyant testing. Ghost Expedition participants were asked to stand up against the storage doors across from the floating staircase which leads to the multiple dining rooms above. Many sensitive people over a two-year period were documented as experiencing a sense of confinement from behind the doors and at times, described various unpleasant odors, not associated with food. In the early days of slavery, shipments of men and women about to be sold by their captors into slavery were contained in the two small storage rooms behind the doors. Often packed to standing capacity only, many perished from the inhumane conditions. Residual energy such as this from the past were noted more often than not.

Cafe Havana, located at 842 Royal Street, was the site of a very simple ISPR investigation. The entity of a young woman haunts the property and communicated without hesitation to the ISPR Team. Most of the paranormal activity in the cigar emporium takes place during after-hours, after the owners lock and leave the premises. It became commonplace for the owners to unlock Cafe Havana in the morning and find that the price stickers on the cigars that fill the large walk-in humidor room are moved around. Obviously, the female entity, who is seen in long sweeping dresses and likes to giggle, isn' t keen on smoking cigars, but she doesn't mind playing with them.

Cafe Beignet, formerly the New Orleans Coffee and Concierge, is located at 334-B Royal Street, right next to the Eighth District Police Station. Cafe Beignet is the site of a persistent residual haunting. The apparition of a young woman with long dark hair and early American Indian attire, is often seen inside the little restaurant after closing hours. The apparition is seen walking from the inside wall, closest to the courtyard, through the empty tables and into the wall that is shared with the art gallery next store. Dr. Montz believes that the hustle and bustle of the small coffee shop during business hours prevents the residual from being noticed by the majority of visitors or employees. But during the evening hours, after the energy settles down inside Cafe Beignet, chances greatly increase to witness the young woman make her routine stroll.

The Chart House Restaurant foyer was a popular location for Ghost Expedition researchers to put the Psi abilities of Ghost Expedition participants to the test.

The Chart House Restaurant is the most recent business on the corner across from Jackson Square. At one time it was a spaghetti factory.

Uptown Haunting

On a fairly quiet street in the Uptown District of New Orleans stands a house on the corner of a block. Vacant for years, according to the surrounding neighbors, the house underwent a major restoration during 1996. On May 1, 1996, the house received its first live tenants in almost a decade. The terrifying activity in the house was documented as early as the first day of residency of the tenants, Jenny and George.

A cleaning crew was hired to scrub the recently-restored house before the new tenants moved in their belongings. Jenny was there to supervise and to pitch in, to expedite the process. Within four hours, the walls, floors, windows and appliances had been scrubbed and left shining. Within the next couple of hours, living room and bedroom furniture was moved in. The two extra bedrooms and dining room were left empty with the exception of boxed books and clothing. The couple's other belongings were left in storage in another state.

Around 2:00 p.m., Jenny and George left their three dogs inside the house and ran to a fast food restaurant to pick up something to eat. Within the half hour, they returned to find little white feathers from an unknown source scattered around the living room and the hallway that runs the length of the house. Not owning anything stuffed with feathers, the couple was puzzled. Because they were so tired from the move, they simply cleaned up the feathers and threw them out. They said that the amount of feathers would have filled a small paper bag.

Jenny and George spent the next several hours readying their bedroom, bathroom and kitchen for normal everyday usage. Nothing unusual occurred until the middle of that night.

At almost 4:00 a.m., the couple was awakened from their sleep by the yelping of one of the three dogs and other noises that they could not decipher. They ran down the hallway to find one of their dogs lying on its side on the hardwood floor in the middle of the living room, spinning in circles without any control. The second dog was yelping helplessly at the other dog's plight. As soon as the couple reached the spinning dog, he came to a complete stop. George and Jenny both scooped up their pets in an effort to comfort them. The comfort was only momentary when Jenny realized that their third dog was missing.

They searched the closets of the three bedrooms, the hallway closet, the dining room. The dog was no where to be found. Terrified and confused, Jenny began to sob when George heard a faint, muffled cry. Straining their ears, the source of the crying was difficult to detect. The only room left was the kitchen, though they had closed the kitchen door and made the three dogs comfortable in the living room before retiring for the night. It seemed impossible but there was nowhere else to look. They turned the knob on the kitchen door and opened it. The muffled crying became more distinct, although there was nothing left to see in the kitchen except the inside of the pantry.

The couple opened the pantry door and was beyond horrified to find their third dog held prisoner inside a taped moving box. From that night on, through the duration of their stay in the house on the corner, the couple kept their bedroom door locked with their three dogs at the foot of their bed.

Throughout the month of May 1996, George and Jenny experienced many unexplained occurrences inside their new home. Objects would disappear, only to be found at a later date in a totally unrelated area. The interior of the house remained cold without the benefit of air conditioning. The moods of the couple, along with those of their pets, changed often for no apparent reason. George and Jenny's new home in the Uptown area of New Orleans was quickly becoming a daily nightmare of large proportions. Strange occurrences happened with increasing frequency. The summer months brought no relief.

The house was vacant for almost ten years before its renovation and subsequent occupation by George and Jenny. New wiring and appliances had been installed by the owner. One of the new features of the home was central air conditioning. However, not once during June, July or August, did the tenants need to use this air conditioning. During a blistering hot summer in New Orleans, complete with almost consistent, 100 percent humidity, the house stayed cool and sometimes even chilly.

New to town, the couple made some new acquaintances. Periodically, they would invite these potential friends to the house to socialize. The couple reported that they never had guests that stayed more than an hour. Guests in the house appeared to be fidgety, uncomfortable, and a few seemed to get a little rude for no apparent reason. The couple also reported that when they made the effort to socialize with these people again, even to make plans to meet outside of their house, almost all of their invitations were turned down with no plans set for a future date.

George and Jenny began to experience problems between one another. Jenny was fighting almost daily bouts of depression which she could not explain. The couple, who claimed that they had only minor disagreements throughout their six-year marriage, were now experiencing incredible arguments which often escalated to the point of breaking material belongings, screaming, and threats of physical harm to each other. During one such argument in mid-June, the couple recalled that Jenny picked up a fork and knife off the kitchen counter and threw them at George, who was standing in the doorway to the hallway.

Bedroom.

The couple's three dogs became unnaturally complacent. They spent most of their time inside of the house usually huddled together under a coffee table in the living room. The couple planned to fence in the backyard for the dogs but never got around to the project. On occasion, the dogs would simultaneously begin to growl and bark out of control. These episodes would take the couple a half an hour or more to settle the dogs down. In the early evening of July 7, 1996, George and Jenny were watching television in the living room with all three dogs lying under the table at their feet. The couple recalled that they began to feel agitated and uncomfortable. Before they had a chance to speak to each other, the dogs began one of their barking fits, this time directed at the empty dining room adjacent to the living room. The couple jumped to their feet facing the dining room. To the right of the room, they both witnessed a large area of space which seemed to wave in and out. It was similar to seeing heat rising off the pavement during a hot day, or in the distance on the sand when the sun is shining brightly. The couple felt the atmosphere become heavy; it was harder for them to breathe. Frightened, the couple froze in the spot where they were standing. The dogs continued to bark in a wild fashion. Within a minute, the atmosphere returned to normal and the wavy atmosphere in that area dissipated. They looked at each other and then

jumped as a huge crash resounded through the house. The couple ran down the hallway and stopped dead in their tracks at the kitchen door. All of the clean dishes, silverware and glasses from the day, which were drying on the counter, were scattered across the floor. The plates and glasses were in pieces everywhere. The rubber dish holder was flipped upside down over some of the broken pieces, several feet from the counter. Day to day, the couple never knew what to expect—what would be broken, what would be missing, what would trigger a serious depression. In late August, George called the ISPR. The investigation took place on September 2, 1996.

When the ISPR Team entered the home, the investigators felt uneasy. The inside temperature of the house was quite cool even though there was no air-conditioning running and the outside temperature was still in the upper eighties. In the front of the house, in the living room and dining room, one of the investigators immediately felt depressed while the others experienced feelings of agitation. When the team moved into the kitchen, the depressed investigator began describing a woman in her mid-thirties with black hair. She described the woman sitting at the kitchen table with a bloodied steak knife, bleeding from both wrists. The investigator began crying and her complexion went very pale. Jenny started to cry. She claimed that everything the investigator was saying felt like a forgotten memory coming back to mind even though she knew those were not her memories.

Livingroom.

Dr. Montz recorded extremely high electro-magnetic readings in the dining room and the kitchen. The meter fluttered without any kind of consistency throughout the two rooms. It was noted too, that the temperature of the kitchen was at least eight degrees cooler that the rest of the house. Although the entire house was unusually cool considering the heat outside and no benefit of air conditioning, the temperature of the remaining rooms stayed relatively the same. Dr. Montz discussed possible options with the couple after the investigation. They seemed to be simultaneously relieved and upset. They couldn't decide what they wanted to do, it was all very overwhelming. They assured them that the property records would be researched and a report would be prepared for them within a week. The plan was agreed.

In the property records from New Orleans City Hall, it was documented that the house was owned for almost one year in 1982 by a married couple. In 1983, another couple bought the house and turned it into a rental property. The local newspaper archives were also researched. In the newspaper that was published two months prior to the sale of the house in 1983, an obituary was discovered for the man who owned the house in 1982, and an obituary for his son. Both had died during an apparent robbery. In a paper published six weeks later, an obituary appeared for the wife. It did not reveal her cause of death. According to some of the neighbors who had lived on the street long enough to know, they informed the ISPR that after the sale of the house, renters moved in and out for a couple of years. The house was then vacant for almost a decade, falling into disrepair and becoming an eyesore on the block. After renovations in early 1996, George and Jenny rented the house and moved in on May 1, 1996.

Four days after the investigation, and after researching the history of the house, the ISPR tried to contact George and Jenny. The phone number had been disconnected. One of the investigators went over to the house to leave a note in the mailbox. As it turned out, there was no need to leave the note, for

the house was empty; there was no evidence of the couple or their dogs. Two days later there was a *for rent* sign on the front door. The investigator called the number and spoke with the owner. She informed the investigator that the couple did not pay their August and September rent and decided to pay the couple a visit in person only to find the house vacant. She said it wasn't the first time this happened and wondered aloud if it would be the last.

Ursuline Convent
1100 Chartres Street

Many years have passed since the Order of Ursuline Nuns has resided here, yet they are still seen walking in procession, descending the old staircase in single file on their way to the chapel. The first Ursuline Nuns landed at this province on August 7, 1727. The original convent was very small and constructed of wood. It stood in front of the present structure, closer to the river. The structure quickly deteriorated, and another convent was needed. Construction began in 1745 and was completed in 1752. The front of the convent faces the river, the rear entrance is on Chartres Street. This convent is actually twenty-five years older than the settling of the United States, and it's the oldest building still standing in the Mississippi Valley. Dr. Montz provides the details:

> Through the passage of time, the great fires of 1788 and 1794 in the French Quarter, the War of 1812, the Civil War and the devastating hurricanes that plagued New Orleans, this religious fortress still stands. The convent has lasted throughout the settling of the New World, specifically the Louisiana Territory, which saw a succession of owners from French, Spanish, back to French and then to Americans.
>
> When I begin an investigation of a building of this nature, I receive no prior information on the building or events of the structure. This method enables me to instruct a team through, without bias. I first met with the curator at the main entrance to the convent. I was then introduced to a caretaker of the property, James. James was instructed to show me and two other Psi investigators through the first and second floors, then to the attic.
>
> Throughout the investigation, I measured several atmospheric changes at times of Psi information. Clairvoyants can sometimes see the energy that remains, kind of like watching a movie or viewing a snapshot of the past. Each person's abilities are different, so each person's abilities manifest in different ways. The clairvoyants could see the energy of the nuns,

dressed in black, their rosaries swaying from their belts as they scurried through the great halls from one room to another. They were assisting confused, crying children who were dressed in ragged, dirty clothing. The consensus was that it was during the War of 1812. The clairvoyants also sensed dark blue uniforms. It was not determined at that point to which time frame the uniforms belonged.

The clairvoyant information was lengthy. They commented on a large procession in the front yard, facing the Mississippi River, with nuns, priests with red hats of some style, dressed in black. There were many people in colorful clothing, horses and carriages, and families; it appeared to be residual impressions of some kind of parade, like Mardi Gras of old. When the curator heard of this, she said, "There was a great procession for the opening of the new convent at this site in 1752! It started at the old convent near Canal Street, stopped at the St. Louis Cathedral, then to the new convent at 1100 Chartres!" She could barely contain her excitement while relaying her confirmations.

The second floor was non-eventful. Most of the rooms are now offices and archives. You could tell there used to be bedrooms and classrooms on this floor. But as we climbed the stairs in the rear of the second floor, up to the attic, the air grew thick and musty. Everyone's heart and pulse rates increased dramatically. James said the only time he has ever had experiences at the convent have all been up in the attic.

Walking through the attic door was like stepping into a time capsule that's been sealed for 245 years. The walls are still in their original condition, built of small slats of dark wood, 2" x 12" x 1/4", attached to 2" x 4"s, unpainted. That adds to the ancient feel of the attic. The massive exposed wooden beams overhead weigh thousands of pounds, holding the structure's roof in place.

Everyone commented on the different feel in the energy in the center room of the attic. It had a nervous energy type of feel. James informed us that this is the same area where he always feels like someone is standing over his shoulder watching him. He said, "Sometimes it seems like I can almost feel the cold breath touching my neck, gives me goose bumps and a cold chill down my back, somebody's watchin' me work." There was a sadness in this area. The presence was determined to be a child who died from illness in one of these attic rooms.

The historical Ursuline Convent is open to visitors.

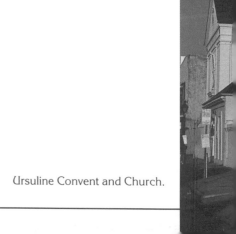

Ursuline Convent and Church.

Ursuline Convent.

U.S.S. *Cabot*

Formerly Docked On The Mississippi River

For six years, the U.S.S. *Cabot*, the last remaining light air craft carrier in existence, sat rusting on the curve of the Mississippi River in New Orleans. The U.S.S. *Cabot* was a motionless reminder of some of the most intense battles of WWII.

The *Cabot*, nicknamed the "Iron Woman" by the most famous WWII correspondent, Ernie Pyle, had earned fame in print and through the overseas radio network. She was active in numerous battles, including the October 1944 sinking of Japan's super battleship, the *Musashi*, during the Battle of Leyte Gulf. She also assisted in the sinking of *Musashi's* sister ship, the Yamato, on April 7, 1945. The *Cabot* suffered many attacks as well.

On November 25, 1944, two kamikaze planes smashed into the catapult control room of the *Cabot*, leaving two large holes in the forward portion of the flight deck and completely wiping out a quad-40mm gun tub, including its radar. The attack killed thirty-five men. Seventeen severely injured men were transferred to a hospital ship. Many more injured remained on board. Fifty-two years later, believing the rumors that the U.S.S. *Cabot* may be haunted, the producers of the television program *Sightings* contacted the ISPR. On August 4, 1996, the ISPR investigation was conducted. The ISPR Team was not informed of any prior paranormal experiences aboard the U.S.S. *Cabot*.

The ISPR Team arrived at the ancient Press Street Wharf around noon. The U.S.S. *Cabot* listed quietly against the dock, a swaying memorial to a more aggressive time. It felt almost intimidating to stand next to the ship and look overhead. The ship's impressive architecture cast a dark shadow for blocks down the wharf. The *Cabot*, currently owned by a foundation, has been docked here for six years. The original plans to convert the ship into a maritime museum fell through; the funds to complete the necessary renovations ran out. Standing on the dock, three of the clairvoyant investigators voiced simultaneously that they would not be alone once aboard the ship.

Fifteen minutes later, the *Sightings* director and his crew arrived at the wharf. Within minutes, a local TV reporter and cameraman arrived. After the interview with Dr. Montz, a foundation representative arrived and warned the team of some of the possible dangers aboard the *Cabot*. With no electricity, therefore no lights, it would be difficult to see the open hatches in the decks. The air had become toxic deep in the ship and some of the lower decks were taking on water. He strongly cautioned the team to stay together. People have been known to get lost below decks. And finally, there was no air conditioning and the day's temperatures were escalating into the mid-90s with 95 percent humidity. This meant the threat of heat exhaustion or worse, heat stroke. It made for interesting conditions under which to film an investigation.

The ISPR Team and the *Sightings* crew unloaded equipment from the vans, which included lights, booms, mics, digital audio recorders, high-eight cameras, TV cameras, magnetometers, and a thermalgraph camera. Dr. Montz recommended that both teams test their equipment; it's common for equipment to fail during investigations. Sure enough, the battery for the high-eight drained as soon as the camera was turned on. The dat deck had three dead batteries. All of the batteries had been charged the night before. The fourth one worked.

It wasn't difficult to climb the ladder at the bow because of the ship's listing toward the dock. Once on board, the hatch door was opened, which is located several decks below the flight deck, and the team entered. The interior of this vast metal ship was pitch black, hot and steamy. The atmosphere had a thick, tangible feel to it. The temperature registered at eighty-nine degrees. As the other investigators followed Dr. Montz and Ed into the ship, followed by the *Sightings* crew, a cold wind rushed through everyone in the corridor. Everyone commented on it. The temperature dropped eighteen degrees for forty-five seconds then returned to eighty-nine degrees. There was a definite independent energy on board. The flashlights created oddly-shaped shadows as the team walked in and out of open hatches clairvoyantly surveying old gray rooms, as Dr. Montz and Ed recorded different kinds of atmospheric readings. The clairvoyant investigators gave their impressions of occurrences that might have taken place in each room.

After traveling only thirty feet into the interior, the entire team again felt something very cold. Michael, a clairvoyant investigator, could see a faint, white colored cloud where it stopped between clairvoyant investigators Jillian and Daena. The image became visible and the three of them described a young man with light-colored hair, wearing what appeared to be dark blue navy attire. When the cameraman swung his camera to face that location, the image faded from the camera lights, the cold spot departed and the temperature returned to normal.

The team continued further into the ship. Suddenly, a variety of clanging noises was heard. In the area near the hanger deck located before the staircase that leads to CIC (Combat Information Center), voices were eminating from the crew quarters on the deck below. Everyone stood still, listening. Many times, recorded sounds and voices are those that can be heard by normal means. We were able to accomplish this during the ISPR investigation of the *Queen Mary* (a luxury liner now docked permanently in Long Beach, California). However, for the investigation of the U.S.S. *Cabot*, all audio equipment, save the TV cameras, had malfunctioned. The TV cameras did not record the voices. Within a minute, the voices ceased.

The heat was beginning to take a its toll, so both team and film crew took a break to get some fresh air outside. It was almost 7:00 p.m. Six hours had passed. During the break, a young woman arrived at the ship. She had witnessed an apparition onboard years before. When the break was over, she

For years, the U.S.S. *Cabot* sat on the Mississippi River
in New Orleans after its return journey from Spain.

joined the group as they made their way to Combat Information Center. The CIC was intact, with all its original equipment. It appeared as though the crew had just walked off and had forgotten to return. As the team entered the CIC, the electro-magnetic energy fields alternated from very low to almost zero, to increases of six miligause. The movement of the EM field also corresponded with the location of an entity as it moved near Daena.

The team moved closer to the center of the ship, which opened up, over-looking the hanger deck, located under the flight deck where the planes were stored. The clairvoyant investigators empathically felt that a serious fire occurred in this area. They continued through the hanger deck to a flight of stairs that led down to the aft of the ship. It was a small area. The next deck down contained living quarters or staterooms. Most remarked that it felt tense and claustrophobic. On the fourth deck down, there was a paneled area with carpeting and in this location, the temperture dropped sharply. This was validated to be the same location where the young woman had encountered the apparition of a sailor, years earlier.

The team entered the crew quarters behind the hatchway and the director announced that he heard voices. Jillian and Michael heard them too. They seemed to emit from a small hatch that led further into the belly of the ship, although that had to be below the waterline. Noise from the waves of the Mississippi River were slapping the side of the ship somewhere above their heads. Everyone waited and listened. The unnatural sounds stopped.

When the team returned to the stairs, Jillian and the young woman felt something push by them. Jillian described a large man in a white uniform with gold braids. It was discoverd later that during an an air attack on the ship, an Admiral was shot aboard the USS *Cabot*. The entity moved on and the team made its way back to the starting point on the bow.

After the tenth hour passed, the equipment was lowered back off the ship. The investigation concluded with a taped interview of the ISPR Team by *Sightings*. They agreed unanimously that the U.S.S. *Cabot* is indeed haunted. The ISPR investigation of the U.S.S. *Cabot* premiered on the television program *Sightings*, on October 11, 1996 and still airs today.

ISPR Parapsychologist Dr. Larry Montz gives a pre-investigation interview for the television series *Sightings*, on the dock next to the U.S.S. *Cabot*.

The flight deck of the U.S.S. *Cabot*.

The ISPR investigators check out the upper decks of the ship during a break.

──────Williams Research Center──────
410 Chartres Street

The Williams Research Center building used to house the Third District Municipal Court. The jail cells and booking station were located on the first floor and the courtroom on the second. Built in 1915, it was functional until 1973. After it closed, the building was vacant for many years. In the early 1990s, the Historic New Orleans Collection, which houses property records for the French Quarter, dating back to the early 1700s, bought the building for its own expansion. The Williams Research Center is named for General and Mrs. L. Kemper Williams. The original Historic New Orleans Collection is still located on Royal Street.

The first order of business for renovations was to gut the entire building. Shortly thereafter, construction crews began complaining of strange occurrences that they could not explain. They were constantly startled by the slamming of jail cell doors that no longer existed and the sight of police officers in outdated blue uniforms, walking the hallways.

Is the building haunted? Technically, yes. By entities? No.

The ISPR labeled the Williams Research Center as a perfect example of a Residual Haunting. No entity is needed for this kind of paranormal activity. A residual haunting can occur when energy from a past event is trapped in the Earth's electro-magnetic field. We don't yet know scientifically exactly how or why this happens. On random occasions, we can see, hear, smell or a combination thereof, some event that took place in the past. This energy can be from a traumatic event or something very mundane that was repeated over and over. It's similar to watching a movie on video tape. The actors are not in your television set, just the recorded images. That's why the scene doesn't change.

Residual hauntings are the foundation for the misconception that entities come back on the anniversary of their murders and re-enact their deaths. That simply is not true. But residuals of such an event could happen during the anniversary, yet it could happen any day of the week, any time of the day. Residual hauntings are also responsible for people believing that they have a ghost in their home that walks the hallway every night at the same time. That too, is a fallacy. Entities don't keep track of the time as we do while we're living, but residual hauntings can occur at the same time of day.

Currently, the only way to rid a property of a residual haunting is still in theory form. Parapsychologists are working on a new laser that could be shot at a residual haunting as it's taking place. The concept is that this would disperse the energy, therefore clearing the property of the residual haunting activity. However, the technology has not been fully developed at this time.

Since residual hauntings are unpredictable, parapsychologist Dr. Larry Montz realizes how slim the chances are of having a laser ready at the time that the residual haunting is taking place. His theory is to blast the entire location with the laser and disrupt the entire field of the property. This is similar to watering an entire plot of land before a fire is ignited in order to prevent the fire from beginning at all.

The construction work on the Williams Research Center has been long completed. It may be that the fields inside the property which generated the previous residual hauntings have been disrupted, for since the opening of the Center, no further paranormal activity has been reported.

Opposite page: The Williams Research Center used to be the Third Precinct Police Station and Second City Criminal Court.

—Other Sites Investigated by the ISPR —

The ISPR was retained to conduct investigations of private properties throughout the state of Louisiana. Here's a partial list of more ISPR investigation properties that you can visit.

Absinthe Bar
Acme Oyster House
Alibi Bar
Andrew Jackson Hotel
Antoine's Restaurant
Arnaud's Restaurant
Audubon Park
Beauregard-Keyes House
Bottom of the Cup Tea Room
Brennan's Restaurant
Chalmette Battlefield
City Park Stadium
Coffee Pot Restaurant
Court of Two Sisters Restaurant
Destrehan Plantation
D.H. Holmes Department Store -Canal Street
8th Precinct Police Station
1850 House Museum
Elms Mansion
Federal Fibre Mills Building
Gallier House
Golden Lantern Bar
Historic New Orleans Collection/Museum
Kerry's Irish Pub
Lafitte's Blacksmith Shop

Lalaurie House
Louisiana Capital Building
Madame John's Legacy House
Marie Laveau Apartments
Metairie Cemetery Legend
Musée Conti Wax Museum
Myrtles Plantation
New Orleans Mint
New Orleans Superdome
Oak Alley Plantation
Olde N'awlins Cookery
Original Jax Brewery
Pat O'Brien's Bar
Playboy Club (former)
Pontchartrain Beach Amusement Park site
Pontalba Buildings
Rosedown Plantation
Steamboat Natchez
Spring Fiesta House
St. Elizabeth's Orphanage
St. Helene Hotel
St. Pierre Hotel
Tulane University
U.S. Customs House
WDSU French Quarter Studios